MANAGING YOUR TEAM

How to Organise People for Maximum Results

JOHN SPENCER
& ADRIAN PRUSS

PIATKUS

Copyright © 1992 John Spencer and Adrian Pruss

First published in 1992 by
Judy Piatkus (Publishers) Ltd
5 Windmill Street
London W1P 1HF

First paperback edition 1993

Reprinted 1996

The moral right of the authors has been asserted

*A catalogue record for this book is available
from the British Library*

ISBN 0–7499–1110–7
ISBN 0–7499–1295–2 (pbk)

Designed by Paul Saunders
Edited by Carol Franklin

Set in 10½/12½ pt Linotron Plantin Light by
Wyvern Typesetting Ltd, Bristol
Printed and bound in Great Britain by
Biddles Ltd, Guildford and King's Lynn

CONTENTS

FOREWORD

The company of today is not the company of yesterday. The attitudes of the managers and entrepreneurs at the opening of the twentieth century were very different from those that are closing that century. The needs of the individuals, and more importantly the recognition that committed, motivated people create more in every respect for their companies is a concept of only the last half of the century. A company where everyone had a place and knew it, where the job was all that mattered and individual expression was for outside work hours, is a museum piece; today a company recognises that it must be an environment where people can develop themselves. Such an attitude pays dividends too, literally. Companies are more productive and more profitable when the employees are 'on the team'.

Where there is no uncertainty about a problem then usually no team is needed; any group with a common purpose can fulfil requirements. It is when levels of uncertainty rise that people need to operate in these highly specialised frameworks we call teams. The fact is that today uncertainty in all aspects of business has risen to the point where many analysts believe we are in constant chaos, in a world of continuous change. Teams are not a luxury, they are the only way forward.

Of the employees who form the teams; gradually rank is being replaced by ability. More people are being promoted not because they are 'the next in line', but because they have shown the aptitude for the job to which they are promoted. Meritocracy is not the established rule yet; but the change is happening. Twenty-five years ago the decision to promote a man 'over somebody else's head' who was next in line would certainly have needed explaining and justifying. It would have been rare, and would almost certainly have resulted in the resignation of the person passed over. Today such a decision might still raise an eyebrow, but little more. But for companies to locate those with skills deserving promotion requires a greater openness than before to allow talent to flourish. And, perhaps more importantly, it has to provide an environment where the person 'passed over' is able still to develop to his or her own limits without feeling 'left behind'. We have not found a way to perfect that yet, but the winds of change are blowing, and blowing for the good. Almost every initiative taken up by the major companies in the world today are designed in some way, at some level, to develop individuals either for their own sake, the company's sake or hopefully for both.

And there is no more significant identity for that change than in the recognition of the team in business. The team has become a sophisticated structure. It is finely engineered, maintained to a high standard, and when running smoothly it is highly productive. It provides an environment in which energy can be maximised towards corporate needs, which also allows for the individual to satisfy his or her own needs within work, rather than only outside of it.

So often seemingly dull, unimaginative and uncreative employees surprised their companies when they revealed the depth of their energy outside work. But it was the corporate attitudes that stifled them, and when released companies recognised they had a pool of talent, a wealth of resources, at their fingertips. This is what we call empowerment.

Teambuilding is not unskilled labour; it is precise engineering to high specification. To bring teams together, to energise them, to give them focus, to motivate them and to mobilise them is not work to be taken lightly. The authors of this book have a depth and a breadth of knowledge in corporate teambuilding that is summarised here. They have applied their principles in practice and they have proven that they work.

Perhaps the most important point to be recognised is that teambuilding is not a destination, it is a journey.

The exercises, checklists and notes throughout the book are practical advice; the authors recommend that they be used rather than just learnt. I recommend that also. A company with well-motivated, well-balanced teams is an effective company. In the modern world an ineffective company will not exist in the long term.

Rod Margree, Managing Director of the Settlement Services
Division of the London Stock Exchange

INTRODUCTION

'The most important thing in the Olympic Games is not winning but taking part . . . the essential thing in life is not conquering but fighting well.'
Pierre de Coubertin in a speech to the Olympic Games 1908

Despite all the reasons usually given for the development of teams in the business environment, the fact is that most people basically prefer to work in teams, at least for much of the time. Working in a group or a department seems to offer security, indeed to some degree it does, and it can be rewarding at a personal as well as a business level. A very quick overview of history soon shows the team structure in evolution.

In prehistoric times our hunter–gatherer ancestors grouped in teams for added security and strength; today's 'loner' in the dog-eat-dog world of the City of London would not have survived long in the sabre-toothed tiger–eat–sabre-toothed tiger world of yesteryear. He would have been killed off by any of a number of dangers that team grouping gives protection against.

People left the caves and moved to structured dwellings, but they still lived in communal houses for protection – most often by then protection from each other!

As society developed, many of those threats were overcome and people were able to work individually, and to build individual dwellings. However, we see immediately that the 'team' surfaced voluntarily. Perhaps Desmond Morris would suggest this was a throwback to our ancestral times; no matter why. The fact is that the local church and local activities became the places where the team was first in evidence.

There were times when teams were necessary for purely practical reasons, for example, it is hard to imagine a self-employed builder being solely responsible for the Pyramids.

Let's move forward in time to Camelot, and the Round Table of King Arthur. Arthur put together an effective team, a team with purpose and direction, united and well led towards the common purpose of defending the kingdom against the Saxon invasions. It was when the kingdom was secured and Arthur's knights sought a new quest – for the Holy Grail – that the team fell apart. Each knight had his own beliefs and needs, and the unity and direction were lost. There are many lessons for the modern business person in the story of Camelot; we shall come to those lessons in due course.

Medieval times saw the creation of the first business teams, the Guilds, formed for the self-protection of the various trades. It is these Guilds that formed the basis of the modern business structures; as business evolved so specialist teams emerged.

History lesson over and the message is clear – the modern business environment is not new; it's just new eyeliner on an old face. Having considered the existence of teams, we must now look at their advantages, without which they would not have thrived.

First, and obviously, individuals simply cannot do some jobs alone – building the Tower of Pisa, the Taj Mahal, the Empire State Building are clear examples. It is not just the quantity of manpower needed; such huge tasks require a variety of skills and disciplines that are beyond one individual to learn or master within one lifetime. Such tasks require the combining of those who have followed different, mutually exclusive, paths. A typical sports team (say, a cricket side) clearly shows the results of combining specialist skills (bowlers, batsmen, fielders and sub-dividing each into even more defined roles such as spin bowlers, and so on).

Also, there are the advantages of synergy and what is known as 10 per cent hitchhiking. Synergy can be summed up as 2 plus 2 equals 5. In other words, when two or more talented people come together they can often produce an energy and creativity that is beyond the simple combination of them both. In 1907 ship-builders, W. J. Pirrie and J. Bruce Ismay, had dinner together and discussed what was then an incredible and futuristic proposition that no doubt increased in grandeur as the two men developed their thinking together; to build three huge ships for trans-

Atlantic crossing that would surpass anything of the day. All three were built; and they were the most resplendent creations afloat. (Not every story has a happy ending, however, since one of the three ships was the Titanic!)

Ten per cent hitchhiking is a part of synergy; it is the basis of a widely-used team technique called brainstorming (which we will look at in detail later), where anyone can make any suggestion to the team towards solving a problem, devising an idea etc. No idea is criticised or rejected, because often from a silly suggestion someone else can pick up (or 'hitchhike') 10 per cent of the idea and build a better one.

The technique of 10 per cent hitchhiking can best be explained from the activity that gives it its name; one person 'picks up' an idea, drives it as far as they can, then drops it off for the next person to pick up, and so on . . . Perhaps only a fragment ('10 per cent') of one person's work can be picked up by the next, but gradually ideas build. From irrationality can come great thinking.

A team can demand more authority to put through its decisions than can an individual. Clearly, an organisation may have more confidence in giving authority to a team knowing that the checks and balances within the structure prevent any one individual implementing their own unworkable ideas. One person alone, focused on one aspect of work, could miss important points that a team would see. (For example, it is rumoured that one architect's plan for a bridge over the St Lawrence Seaway was stopped in the nick of time – he had based the height of the proposed bridge on the *average* height of ships using the waterway!)

Since much authority is delegated, those with power prefer to delegate it to teams rather than individuals, lest the successful individual should retain too much of the power, and surpass his or her own superiors. Powerful teams can at least be broken up and their threatening power thus dispersed.

Teams take more risks than individuals. They have a natural protection – you can sack a man (as a scapegoat or otherwise), but you can't (usually!) sack the whole team. Risk taking is a necessary and normal part of business. The team structure provides the authority to take the risks, the dare to do so, and the balance of strengths and capabilities that give the wisdom to take reasonable risks, rather than unreasonable ones. The Channel Tunnel venture is a consortium of many financial and physical resources precisely because no one individual company (and certainly no individual) would be sensible in taking the risk alone, even if it had the resources to do so. The checks and balances in the system have almost certainly paved the way for the continued success of this remarkable project.

Teams can be self-motivating. If the team is put together in a balanced way then it creates its own dynamics, and it drives itself. Individuals suffer from lack of motivation for a variety of reasons; teams can overcome it more easily. The means of getting proper balance and good leadership are important in team building and will be discussed in the early chapters of the book.

A team is made up of a variety of individual people, all with their own spheres of influence within the company. Consequently, the team as a whole has a deeper access to the organisation structures than any one individual. The Civil Service provides an obvious example of this; they say that when the rest of civilisation has joined the dinosaurs the Civil Service will still be going strong!

Teams have greater access to communications than individuals. Information both to and from the team is usually more structured, with a consequence that implementation of team decisions is more effective.

Teams have a more progressive learning curve than individuals. In other words, teams learn faster. Training is more available, areas of specialisation develop more quickly. Even a basic survey of the development of the American Space Programme – and its spin-offs – shows the potency of specialist teams learning in new fields.

Teams spread a feeling of unity and the sharing of success. This is generally good for the organisation's morale and creates for many a sense of belonging and increased job satisfaction. When job application forms ask if the applicant plays football or cricket the company is not usually greatly concerned to encourage those particular activities, rather it wants to know whether or not the applicant is a 'team player'. Answers like, 'No – I prefer computer games because it keeps other people away from me' are – today more than ever – unlikely to get you the job.

It must be stressed that the advantages noted above are only found where the team is well led and properly structured. Poorly focused, badly led and imbalanced teams can lead to defeat even in the face of victory. However, even when going well, teams can have disadvantages, some of which are listed below.

Team decisions must involve some compromise and possibly some loss of individual genius or flair. This is inevitable, and it is a loss that cannot be resolved within the team structure. However, a well-managed organisation will also have structures that allow flair and genius to surface in other ways – and those that suppress such individuals will simply find their best men 'head-hunted' by the opposition.

Unfortunately, teams can become self-electing oligarchies; often electing people to their number on the basis of likes rather than needs. This problem is usually dealt with in modern teams by the introduction of external consultants who are there as '*agents provocateurs*'; having no specific company loyalty they can challenge what a company employee might feel unable to question.

Sometimes this can have dramatic effects, as in the case of one company for which we have acted as consultants. The company was managed by two directors near retirement, with their two sons on the board, but effectively waiting in the wings. The company was deadlocked into a lack of progress; and it had lost its creative forces. The board could not decide on the correct course of action; it was the external consultants who made clear that the necessary course was to get rid of the first generation directors and replace the management with the 'new blood'. In hindsight, all the members of the board – including the older ones – had recognised this problem, they were simply unable to face implementing it.

Although teams can be self-motivating, as described above, they can also be harder to motivate from outside on those occasions when they lose their driving force. Usually, in these circumstances, it is left to external consultants to inject the new drive, and often this is done with what are kindly called 'job losses'. They say that impending execution focuses the mind wonderfully.

There can be a tendency for some individuals to use the team to highlight themselves, scoring points over other members of the team as a short cut to promotion. In a fair and just world people would never get away with this injustice; in fact it works all too well. This book at least gives team members guidance on how to deal with such problems.

The disadvantages are real, and must be addressed. This book is partly a guide which team members and team leaders can use to reduce the damaging effects of these problems.

In order to understand team dynamics this book draws from our experiences of many types of teams from the business world such as boards of directors, audit teams, management groups, consulting task-forces and so on, but also specialist teams including the following.

Networking teams

These are less formal associations of managers etc., normally from similar positions of authority within an organisation who communicate ('network') with each other across divisional and even corporate boundaries (between different companies). Such associations are becoming more frequent in larger organisations, particularly multinationals. These 'teams' are often the result of people who have worked together in the past in more formal teams (or in the same companies) and they 'maintain their contacts' after leaving.

Hit teams (or 'quick response' teams)

These are formed for a specific purpose, usually for a short duration. They are normally highly mobile, travelling to areas of difficulty whenever needed. On arriving at a site they usually form the nucleus of a larger 'local' team and are often used to energise old and tired teams. They amount to the business world's equivalent of police SWAT (special weapons and tactics) teams.

Strategy teams

These are composed of specialists and people of great experience to whom longer-term and strategic issues are continually referred. In earlier days they would have been called 'think tanks'; using corporate planning tools they apply strategy to new ideas creation, often handing down tactical plans to networking teams or CAT teams (see below).

We have observed that the decision-making process often has to be authorised by line-management; strategy teams sometimes have no authority of their own, other than simply to recommend alternatives.

CAT teams (corrective action teams)

These are one of the tools used in total quality management (TQM). They are problem-solving teams with the authority to implement action on problems referred to them by work groups. They are normally a cross-section of experts and line-management. They exist only as long as the problem they are solving, and individuals will often find themselves on more than one CAT team at a time.

We also draw on the dynamics of other – non-business – teams such as orchestras, acting companies and so on.

In the case of the performing arts, business has failed to realise that for many decades this profession has been solving a modern-day business problem – how to put together an effective team quickly, ready to get immediate results, capable of working together with harmony, and still able to split up and re-group into other teams for later assignments. Special techniques and special energies are needed, and they can be learned and harnessed by following the practical steps outlined in this book.

The authors of this book are at the forefront of consultancy which brings together business people and members of the performing arts in training teams designed to bring just those energies to organisations – with remarkable results.

The book also considers the impact of different cultural backgrounds to teams; team decision-making in Japan, for example, is quite different from its Western counterpart. Both the authors have experience of working with these alternative techniques and there is much that can be learned in order that the modern organisation's teams can benefit from the best of both worlds.

This book is a practical guide for anyone involved in teams, either as a leader or player. It contains practical advice, but also game structures, questionnaires and checklists that allow for continuous development over years.

Teambuilding is not logical, it is psychological. As such, we are dealing with the needs of individuals, their strengths and weaknesses, their desires, their fears and so on. The organisation that believes a team of eight is just eight people is preparing the way for its own demise. Such a team is made up of eight individuals; modern teambuilding is a matter of recognising that and bringing those individuals together in a way that creates the synergy vital to the organisation's own needs – where one times eight equals ten plus, and where the organisation derives what it needs from the team, without taking it away from the individuals.

The modern business environment is also one in a state of continuous flux – management during continuous change. Long-serving teams (so often the ideal of standard 'teambuilding' books) are no longer able to deal with the rapidly changing dynamics of the modern business world. Quick response, corrective action and network teams are needed to respond to the modern environment. This book shows the techniques needed to produce such teams, and from where and how to harness the energies needed. It is unique – the combination of styles of teambuilding from business and non-business environments makes this a book of modern teambuilding for today's needs.

1. THE TEAM CONTRACT

'My people and I have come to an agreement which satisfies us both. They are to say what they please, and I am to do what I please.'

Frederick the Great, King of Prussia

Every team should have, and has the right to have, clear reasons why it exists. It must also have knowledge of when and why it will cease to exist. These reasons are embodied in what is referred to as the 'team contract'. This is not a formal document; indeed it is not a document at all usually, but is a commitment between the team and the people who brought it into existence, and it gives the team its authority to act. Only in a culture of mistrust, often due to history, do we find that teams insist on written rules as to their powers, authorities and specific direction. As we shall see later, in an empowered organisation where clear tasks, goals and objectives are communicated through the team leader to the team, it is not necessary to reduce contracts to writing thereby increasing and reinforcing the empowerment process.

There may be many different types of contracts existing between the team and the business systems, internal and external, within which the team has to operate, but it is sufficient at this point to consider three generic groupings.

1. The contract between the team leader and the members of the team; also the team members with respect to each other. These should not be in conflict because the team leader's responsibility is to identify him or herself with, and only with, the team.
2. The contract with management. The team contract with

19

management having already stated, now, that the team leader divorces from management and identifies him or herself with the team for the sake of the process means that the team leader, with the team, are now one entity.

3. The contract with the outside world. This means that the team has to recognise that it is not purely operating for itself or for management, but that it has a responsibility to the outside world which, in this instance, can include customers, suppliers, other teams, the environment and any interested parties who will be directly or indirectly affected by the decisions and actions of the team (often referred to as stake-holders).

For the team to be effective, its contractual relationships must be established at the outset. Although the contractual relationships can change over a period, if there is not some existing structure from the beginning, then there is a clear sign that the team has not been brought into being on a well thought-out basis and that almost certainly it will lack clear objectives. Indeed, such contracts are not written in stone and *should* change over time as the team moves through its learning process, but they must evolve from a solid foundation; the foundations are the goals and objectives of the team and sight of them should not be lost.

We will now look in more detail at the three generic groupings.

Contract between team's leader and members; also between members

We can describe these contracts as non-negotiable ground rules, to be summarised as follows.

Openness

It is essential that the team leader, with the team members, are as open and honest as they can possibly be when they are discussing their thoughts and feelings concerning the tasks on hand. Later in the book we will be referring back to this concept of openness and how this can be encouraged as it is an essential prerequisite of building and uniting a team. In fact, teambuilding insists on honesty and openness, and allowing team members to disregard the politics, rivalries and other hindrances to teamwork.

Eliminate fantasy

It is essential that fantasy, as we shall see later, is confined to constructive brainstorming. In teamwork, fantasy must be eliminated by discussing accepted facts and not making assumptions (and presenting them as facts), because they cannot – at that point – be checked upon by fellow team members. This is particularly relevant where stronger members of the team act as devil's advocate by presenting fantasy as fact, but then fail to openly distinguish the difference in what they have done to weaker, or less knowlegeable, team members who are unable to challenge their statements.

Respect others' opinions

In order that mutual respect of other team members' opinions can exist it is necessary that team members understand their own values and prejudices. We shall later be considering the issues and the processes by which we, as team members, can understand and accept the differences in attitudes, opinions and behaviours of others. The overriding concept must be the maxim that 'we may not like what people feel or say, but we respect their right to communicate it'.

Be in the 'here and now'

Henry Ford said, 'History is more or less bunk'. Perhaps so, but history can teach us a great deal because it reminds us what other people did in particular situations, with the information at their disposal. But team contracts must look to the future. Team learning is about acknowledging the past, but using that knowledge in the present and perceived future situations. Therefore, one of the ground rules is that the team, with the team leader, must always live in the present with an eye to the future.

Be constructive with your feedback

In any team situation it is very easy to 'knock' the ideas of team members either individually or collectively; this is not helpful for the development of the group. Constructive criticism is descriptive, it relates back to the individual exactly how you have interepreted what they have said and suggests possible consequences that might arise. For instance, if somebody suggests something, look for three positive outcomes before describing a negative consequence and discuss with them their view of the positive elements before discussing those negative possibilities. This shows a desire to reach a consensus without sacrificing principles or major issues.

Be willing to take risks

As we shall see in later chapters, we learn very little from success (except how to repeat it), but we learn a great deal more from so-called failure. Teams are formed to solve problems, identify issues, formulate plans and so on. For this reason we cannot always predict success or failure, but every team must be given the opportunity to work towards success without being castigated for the *partial success*, which in business we unfortunately call failure.

Participate

Teams members are not spectators; they are participants in the game. For this reason it is the team leader's responsibility, a theme we shall develop later, to demand 'hands on' participation from all team members; they cannot observe from the sidelines. Passive observation may be interesting, but coaching participation will develop those team members actively seeking results.

Communicate facts and opinions

Make sure you understand the difference between the two, and that the people you are communicating with can also appreciate the difference. They can respond with their own opinions on facts, and understand your viewpoints from your opinions. If you state opinions as if they were facts, people will make wrong decisions, believing options to be closed which are in fact open – the truth being that they are only closed to your mind.

Be responsible towards the goals

It is the duty of the team leader, jointly with the team members, to be totally responsible towards the tasks and objectives as set and agreed. This means not only allocating expertise, professionalism and energy to the tasks, but also participating at the functional level. For example, if you take on the responsibility of governor of a school, it is essential that you turn up for all the meetings, or recognise when you have lost interest and make way for those who do have the appropriate application.

Be receptive

Receptiveness is not only the ability to listen, but also to accept criticism and challenge. Active listening and recognising what people say is more important than passive acceptance of the team view. Just because we don't like what people are suggesting does not mean that it is not an interesting idea and potentially a fruitful experience.

The contract with management

The team's contract with management amounts to its terms of reference. In order that the team can be effectively motivated, it must know from the outset that it has the authority to implement its decisions. Management has a duty to ensure that it has sufficient authority, and not excessive authority, in this regard. There are many aspects which must be considered in negotiating an effective team contract.

First, there must be disclosure of the boundary rules on the part of both management and the team members.

The definition of boundary rules would include:

● what management expect of them, and why they expect it;
● what the team honestly believes it can do;

- areas that the team potentially feel uncomfortable with;
- areas that management do not want the team to look at, in other words the areas that management are uncomfortable with;
- areas that the team and management feel are acceptable, but which will challenge existing work practices or agreements, perhaps union or health and safety issues.

Secondly, assumptions on both parts must be replaced with certain knowledge on a need-to-know basis rather than a nice-to-know basis. In other words, both the team and management must agree on a set of clearly defined objectives based on the requirements which have brought the team into being in the first place. Quite often teams continue for some time to operate on ill-defined assumptions until it becomes apparent to the team that they are not fulfilling management's requirements and management discovers, albeit belatedly, that the team is not fulfilling the brief it thought it had.

Thirdly, there must be a commitment by management to respond to the team's input. This must be a true commitment and not simply a commitment in words only; all too often we see a commitment by mouth only, and not by action. The team must ensure that its work is being implemented, or understand fully why it cannot be.

Fourthly, there must be free communication within the company on both a horizontal and vertical basis. In other words the team must have access to a flow of information on a hierarchical (vertical) basis, i.e. from the board of directors through to the shopfloor and vice versa; also on a horizontal basis between similar levels of management and indeed between similar operating teams. Such communication must be guaranteed for both input and output of information.

Fifthly, the team must be empowered to seek and find information across the existing management structures. The communication aspect of empowerment means that the team must be clearly shown where their work adds value to the company, where their efforts will show results and where their work fits in with the company's objectives.

Finally, management must communicate the organisation's core values openly. These can be summed up as follows.

- There must be clear statements of requirements, and the reasons for those requirements. In other words, the corporate vision must be understood by all members of the team who can then see their work within a proper perspective inside the company. If the company has a corporate statement – a one-line motto embodying the vision for all to be guided by – then the team must see that its work is conducted within that statement and is directed towards the corporate goals.

- Honesty, integrity, trust and respect. The team must be created for genuine and not cynical or manipulative purposes. If the team, for example, is created only to share their management's own risk taking, then it will be very clearly seen as simply a rubber-stamping body for those decisions and will lose its empowerment to act within the company, as it loses the respect of other teams within the organisation.

- Recognise contribution and give reward. The team must know what the corporate goals are in respect of performance and must know what its rewards will be for maintaining or exceeding performance. These rewards to the team must be stated beforehand to avoid undue expectations and the demotivation that would result should those expectations not be fulfilled. In a simple way football teams, for example, are paid bonuses for winning important games. Corporate teams may receive very practical rewards in a financial form or, perhaps more usually, may receive recognition by the advancement of team members. It may even be something as basic as – in one case – a 'Dutch dash', where an entire team was boat-loaded off to Holland for a weekend of 'lively' celebrations!

- Walk as you talk. Management must be seen to act as it claims it will act. If it makes certain claims verbally, or indeed on paper, but continually fails to live up to those by failing to implement team decisions etc., then the team will see that its efforts are meaningless. This is perhaps the commonest failure of team contracts and can be summed up by team members saying something to the effect of, 'We have many meetings, we thrash out particular problems, we make our recommendations to management but nothing ever gets done . . .'. The team should not be discussing or attempting to implement something which management knows it does not have the authority to deal with and it would appear that the team contract would be faulty from the start were the team to be doing this.

- Professionalism. The company, and therefore the team, must demonstrate a duty of care to its stake-holders, a duty of care to the job in hand, and there must be a recognition and a resolving of conflicts of interest. An example of a regulation enforcing standards of professionalism exists within the Institute of Chartered Accountants in England and Wales, which does not allow an audit practice to receive more than a fixed percentage of its fees from any one client. In other words no client can then effectively 'blackmail' the audit company into 'seeing things the company's way' or threatening to remove the audit at possible great financial loss to the accountants. The duty of care can be critical with good reason; a doctor telling you to lose weight, or give up smoking and drinking, is doing so for mutual benefit – your health and your doctor's application of limited resources; when you are not spending time in the surgery then doctors are free to attend to other, perhaps more needy, cases.

- Reliability of information systems. Teams require information and they must know that the company's information flow is operating effectively. Furthermore, and perhaps most importantly, the team must be able either to circumvent or change bad systems where it discovers them, or it will hit brick walls and nothing will happen.

- Fickle and non-discriminatory behaviour. There are certain particular aspects of the company's behaviour which put the corporate integrity on show, for example its policies towards the disabled and ethnic minorities. Because of public focus on these particular aspects the company's attitude towards them will give away some of its attitude towards all its employees. Non-discriminatory behaviour can also apply to hierarchical behaviour; for example employees might rightfully feel downgraded if they are always required to take the train or tube, while management is empowered to take hire cars and taxis. If the company has good reason for such discrimination then it should make it clear from the outset and it should do so with the agreement of all parties. Since the only realistic argument is likely to be cost-effectiveness and since this is not likely to impress anyone enough to make them flock towards the bus stops, this may well be a difficult argument to sustain.

- Loyalty and commitment. The company must be supportive of the team and committed to it if it expects the team to show equal loyalty and commitment back to the company.

- Openness. There should not be hidden agendas and there must be an open door policy. The team must have sufficient access to higher managerial levels in order to do the job and must in turn allow access to itself from subordinate levels and other interested parties, such as suppliers, customers and so on.

The contract with the outside world

Clearly the team cannot negotiate a contract with all and sundry in the outside world because most of these contracts are implied by social custom; none the less it must recognise from the outset that it has many 'contracts' with a wider relationship than its own company. For example, a large petro-chemical refinery situated near a major town has an implied contract of duty of care to the citizens of that town. If the established operations of the refinery require, and have, a 'fallout zone' of, say, half a mile around the refinery into which the town does not expand, then the refinery also has a duty not to alter its operations to the point where, say, a fallout zone of several miles would be required which would obviously endanger the lives of those then living in it. Conversely, the local community has a duty of care not to build houses up to the factory's fence.

More topically, all companies have a duty of care to the environment, and indeed there is enormous public and governmental pressure on companies to respond favourably to the environment, to the point where there may soon be financial advantages for those who are and financial penalties for those who are not environmentally friendly. An example of a failure of contract between the company and the outside world exists when unacceptable wastes are flushed into local rivers causing illnesses in the locality or damage to local industries, agriculture etc. The reaction from the local community and pressure from the media represents the penalty for failing in this contract. Clearly, this contract exists between the company and the outside world, and not specifically with one individual team within the company, but the team has a duty to act in accordance with that wider contract.

Effectiveness checklist

Teams can consider the effectiveness of their existing contracts by considering the three checklists that follow. Each is designed to analyse the three categories of contracts that were examined above.

Contract between team's leader and members; also between members

This can be completed by any member of the team, including the leader, and is designed to ask the question, 'Is my team's own internal contract effective?'

Key: Ring the number between 1 and 4 which most appropriately answers the question on the basis of:

   1 = No
   2 = To a lesser degree
   3 = To a greater degree
   4 = Yes

1. Can I be honest and open with my fellow team members?   1 2 3 4

2. Do I respect my fellow team members' opinions?   1 2 3 4

3. Am I willing to communicate my thoughts and opinions to others in the team?   1 2 3 4

4. Do I encourage my team to take risks?   1 2 3 4

5. Do I focus on the present as opposed to the past?   1 2 3 4

6. Am I constructive in my feedback?   1 2 3 4

7. Do I believe that my fellow team members are
open and honest with me?   1 2 3 4

8. Do I treat my fellow team members in an adult
and mature way?   1 2 3 4

9. Do I regard myself as an active participant in the
team?   1 2 3 4

Results analysis:

A low score, between 9 and 17, suggests that you are unsure how
to work as a member of a team. It may also indicate a newly
formed team where the members have not yet had the opportunity to develop their relationships. Monitoring the results over a
period of time will either, therefore, show the progress of you as a
team player, or of the team as an entity. As a challenge to yourself, you should ask the questions (a) 'What contribution do I
want to make to the team?' and (b) 'What contribution am I
presently making?'.

A medium score of 18 to 27, suggests, generally, that you are
reasonably developed as a team player, but probably playing in a
team that is not yet unified. There will be occasions when this
score indicates a new member being introduced to an established
team and not yet 'knowing the ropes'. You, as an individual,
should be able to identify which circumstances fit your situation.
The action to be taken will vary according to that answer, but
since there is a basis of strength either in the team or in you,
progress is assured providing there is a commitment on your part.

A high score, of 27 to 36, indicates both commitment on your
part, and an open and well-developed team within which you are
operating. Complacency is the main danger here; repeat these
tests regularly and if the scores significantly fall, then identify
which questions are giving rise to deteriorating answers and
address them. If the deterioration is general, then the team is
losing its commitment and a degree of honest introspection is
called for by the team collectively.

The contract with management

This can be completed by any member of the team and is designed to consider the effectiveness of the team's existing contracts with management. The same 1 to 4 scale is used as with the former checklist.

1. Do I really know the true purpose of my team?   1 2 3 4

2. Am I sure of senior management's commitment?   1 2 3 4

3. Have we got sufficient resources to do the job?   1 2 3 4

4. Do we have effective lines of communication?   1 2 3 4

5. Will management recognise and reward success?   1 2 3 4

6. Do we know why management has delegated this task to us?   1 2 3 4

7. Are we empowered to do the job?   1 2 3 4

8. Will management join us in the tasks to be undertaken, and be part of the work at the functional level?   1 2 3 4

9. Will management honour the contract, come what may?   1 2 3 4

10. Do we get resource and budgetary authorisations with the least difficulty?   1 2 3 4

11. Does senior management know we even *exist*?   1 2 3 4

Results analysis:

A low score, of between 11 to 21, suggests that you are unsure of senior management's commitment to the team and its objectives. This will inhibit the team's ability to recommend courses of action that at first sight would appear to challenge management. It might also suggest that, although management's commitment might be strong, they have failed to communicate that effectively to the team. Either way, it is time for a head-to-head with management with a view to possibly renegotiating, or at least reviewing, the team's basic contract.

A medium score, of 22 to 32, probably indicates that both the team and management are satisfied that both are fulfilling the original contract; however the fact that you have withheld higher scores may suggest that there is a barrier to the team pushing the boundary limits – that the team is unsure of how management will react if it becomes proactive rather than reactive, as it probably is at present. This compromise stage is detrimental as it holds back creativity and it will take effort, and risk, on the part of the team to develop further. It is quite likely that management will appreciate the additional drive, but if not then it is certainly time to address the terms of that original contract so that both management and the team are again certain of exactly what it is they do want from each other.

A high score, of 33 to 44. Congratulations! You and management are in good harmony and this is a very important state for real progress. Maintenance is ever important; monitor and address issues should they later arise to threaten that situation. One word of caution, however, since you are *so* in tune with management, can others in the company tell you from them?

The contract between our company and the outside world

This can be completed by any member of the team and is designed to consider the larger environment in which the team is working, i.e. the company and its relationship with the world at large.

The same scale of 1 to 4 applies as in the previous two checklists.

1. Do we invite external people to the team meetings (i.e. customers, suppliers, the press etc.)?   1 2 3 4

2. Do we visit our customers in order to understand how our goods or services are used in their organisation?   1 2 3 4

3. Do we visit our suppliers to see if what they deliver to us fits into our work processes (i.e. food retail supplier checks)? 1 2 3 4

4. Do we readily identify as a team with the published image of the organisation? 1 2 3 4

5. Do we achieve the necessary permissions and authorisations with the minimum of fuss (i.e. planning permission)? 1 2 3 4

6. Do we admit and publicise our mistakes? 1 2 3 4

Results analysis:

A low score, of 6 to 11, suggests an unwillingness to involve the outside world, or communicate with it. This would indicate a lack of belief in what you are doing (i.e. production or services) and perhaps that you have not thought through the benefits to the community at large. Have you got something to hide? This attitude, in the long run, will demotivate the team and certainly reduce its ability to promote change.

A medium score, of 12 to 17, suggests that both the organisation and the community are unsure of themselves and both probably see each other as an equal *threat*, rather than an equal *opportunity*. An important point to remember here is that it is not this mid-range score that is important, but rather the results over a time-series. If the score represents a constant improvement over previous results, then even if there is a long way to go to develop relationships with the community, the willingness is there. A falling score, however, indicates a deterioration of a once good relationship. In this latter case the team might ask itself whether any new activities on the part of the company are causing that lack of trust to arise.

A high score, of 18 to 24. There is no doubt that you have a healthy attitude towards the important partnerships you value between your customers and suppliers, and that you have a responsible attitude towards the world around and beyond the factory gates. And, equally important, this is being recognised and communicated.

A note of caution
Remember that these questionnaires have been completed with introspection. Would your other team members, your management and the world at large give equal results if they were filling it in?

When team contracts fail

'She knows there's no success like failure and that failure's no success at all.'

Bob Dylan

We often learn very little from success, but everything from failure. If this is true then why do we praise teams for success and punish teams for failure? Will this not encourage teams only to concentrate their energies on things they can win at? Probably the reasons for this attitude are inherent in our society where winning and survival have become synonymous. We are taught that the world loves a winner; and that first is first and second is nowhere. In our schooling and sports we encourage, if not demand, winners. Businesses are trying to install empowerment into their organisations, i.e. giving people more responsibility and asking them to test the corporate boundary limits. At the same time we are asking staff to be more entrepreneurial, and take more risks, but in our discussions with employees they say that if they empower themselves they are called trouble-makers, and if they take entrepreneurial risks and fail, or partially fail, then they are ranked as failures.

Field Marshal Montgomery, who was undoubtedly one of Britain's greatest military commanders, said to his generals, after the Battle of Arnhem, 'It was just one bridge too far'. He did not punish failure, he put the most positive position on it he could.

Similarly, in our businesses, it is time to take a different attitude towards so-called failure, because if we don't then our staff will be increasingly unwilling to take risks and will become stale, inert and put off all but the easiest decisions, or just simply delegate upwards, which seems to be the commonest method at present.

33

There is no simple answer to why some teams succeed and others fail. Countless studies of both winning and losing teams have failed to come up with any criteria that can be used in other situations. Businesses can hold as many post-mortems as they like, but we never learn any practical lessons from them apart from 'Let's do it the same way again', or 'Don't do that again'. In fact, on that basis success can actually become stagnating for a company, stunting its growth, because of the pressure simply to repeat the success rather than to try out new ideas, some of which could lead to even greater success and development.

From our experience teams fail because they have not negotiated effective contracts in the first place. Most, if not all, teams start with the energy and enthusiasm to do the task only to find out, often quite quickly, that they do not have the wherewithal to do the job effectively and therefore to succeed. This is often due to the external factors that influence the team. These external factors – management, unions, environment, economy, fashion etc. – can very quickly influence or indeed destroy an outwardly good-looking team contract.

We have already discussed how to negotiate an effective team contract. What then goes wrong? Why does the team fail and what can we learn from the failure?

In any negotiations of a team contract, between say the team and management, the contract looks rosy at day one, and we can describe this as uninformed optimism. Up to this point the team has concentrated its energies into agreement with management and the team is fired up, and the prevailing attitude is 'Let's get on with the job'. (Often described as 'Never mind the ball let's get on with the game'.) Some time into the process, however, pessimism begins to rear its head. The team begins to discover the inherent blocking mechanisms in the organisation, that prevent it from doing the job. The team comes up against power blocks that do not want the team contract to survive in its present form. Management, on learning more of what's happening, begins to get frightened of the ramifications of the possible outcomes of the team's work, and starts drawing fences around the team. The team then finds itself in a chaotic world, and excuses in the form of key issues are used against them. Such key issues can be described as economic, environmental, investment payback and so on. These may all be pertinent and correct, but if they are they should have been drawn out and discussed during the formation of the team contract, not ignored at that time.

Once the white cells of the organisation begin to cluster around the red-blooded team, the energy of the team begins to wane, and the team starts to report partial failure on its road to demise.

How then can teams 'beef up' the team contracts with management and other interested parties? The answer is that team leaders with their teams must really understand the culture of the organisation. By free and frank discussion with management or people outside the company they must establish the core values of the organisation and others that underpin the team contracts. The organisation's core values, like society's, are very difficult to tease out. Like an iceberg, we only see the tip. For this reason very bland core values are often communicated to our staff, and we apply differing sets of core values to different countries, regions and areas. For example, how can a team based in London agree a set of values on which to build a factory in central Africa? Why should the team contract work in a region that has a completely separate value system, where, say, employment leading to wealth has more importance than environmental issues?

In essence the team must establish whether or not management has the courage to do what they say they are going to do, or are they just going to change their minds when the going gets tough?

In the early 1980s one of us was working as a productivity consultant in a team for an American hospital group. The bed occupancy rates had gone down and the group needed to introduce cost savings. Using quite simple techniques we, as a team, were able to identify surplus administrative staff, including some senior vice presidents. As a team we regularly submitted our cost-saving proposals to the executive board of the hospital. On our advice people were duly removed from senior and middle management positions and we claimed them as staff savings. In fact, the group did not save much money at all, as when we identified people that were no longer needed, they were being offered alternative jobs as gardeners or porters with very little loss of salary. Why? The answer was simple; the hospital group was founded and run by a religious organisation, and it was against their beliefs (i.e. their core values) to sack people. The lesson was quickly learned; you cannot negotiate an effective team contract if at some later stage you will come up against core values of the organisation that were missed at the start. Had this particular core value been fully recognised at the outset then the consultancy would have approached its work quite differently.

So to avoid the failure of team contracts we must understand, and write, team contracts within the core values and the culture of the organisations. These must also be fully communicated.

Let us now look at what we regard as failure. In business different interest groups may have quite different definitions of what constitutes success or failure. In the 1980s, during a period of low interest rates, economic optimism and the continuing bull market, we saw an increase in the number and scale of takeover activities. What appeared at the time to be great successes, by the early 1990s appear to be less so. Polly Peck, Coloroll, British and Commonwealth, and Brent Walker are a few names that come to mind.

In due course, once the administrators and receivers have published their findings, we will, with hindsight, be able to pinpoint certain events, and happenings, within or beyond those companies' control that led to their failure. In the meantime what we can see is the failure of the team's contracts with their suppliers, bankers and creditors etc., who had differing ideas of success and failure that had obviously not been negotiated at the outset of the contract.

Like the example above, then, team contracts can fail because management loses faith or patience with the team. That's not always failure, it's often pulling the rug; management deciding to cut its losses in the light of new evidence. The team is not at fault if the team has done what it negotiated to do. Are teams at fault if, having been encouraged to borrow money at cheap rates, they find themselves in trouble because the government decides to move the goal posts? Daily we hear examples of business people having to manage their way out of difficulty because the team contract between government and business has failed. Is it any wonder that business demanded the ERM (exchange rate mechanism) and other similar vehicles that will iron out the exchange fluctuations of successive government policies.

Teams in business and other organisations must realise that so-called failure of the team is often a result of someone changing the rules. This being so, the teams must not be branded with the hot 'F' for failure, they must be given credibility for work done up to the change in circumstances that led to eventual so-called failure, and be able to use the new information when writing new team contracts.

All failure can be an opportunity to learn to manage the new rules for the next time. Tom Peters, in his book *Thriving on Chaos*, makes the point that increasing success can only happen by increasing failure. Indeed, it is recognised that if you have not enjoyed enough success in business it may well be because you have not yet 'enjoyed' enough failure.

We hear of many instances of teams who negotiate faulty contracts knowingly. In one company we have worked with, the team wished to embark on a new capital project and, having done their sums, worked out that the project budget had to be £286,000. The team knew that the authorisation limit of the MD for capital work was £250,000. Instead of correctly negotiating £286,000, which would have meant a bit more effort, and having to go to head office for authorisation, they fudged the figures to £247,000, knowing it was not enough. As the team leader said, 'When we get to £247,000 with 90 per cent built, who is going to say no?' In fact the plant was built at a cost of £380,000. But if £380,000 is not a viable figure for the payback period demanded – and if all the teams in the organisation did the same – eventually the company would go out of business. In the example above the team appeared outwardly to negotiate an effective team contract; in fact the team contract failed as the team did not build the plant within its stated budget.

Companies' teams, to our mind, do not deliberately set out to negotiate team contracts that fail. They often, however, negotiate within a culture that will breed failure, because the teams – in order to negotiate any meaningful form of contract – will have to bend the rules. The only way out of this problem is to raise the level of empowerment in the organisation that then makes rules only a guideline. Entrepreneurial management can then make and accept occasional forays outside the boundary conditions.

Team leaders, with their teams, for their part must increase their level of honesty and integrity, and appreciate with the organisation that failure is the child of success. We must recognise that all too often the competitive desire to win at any price is the path to failure, whereas failure in an empowered situation can become the road to success.

2. THE TEAM ROLES

'If you have great talents, industry will improve them: if you have but moderate abilities industry will supply their deficiency.'

Joshua Reynolds

The French expression *raison d'être* means, literally, reason to exist or reason for being; unfortunately there is no perfect equivalent in the English language. The slightly less adequate expression that we have used over the years is 'team mission', to refer to more than simply the goals of the team, but also the reasons for its being brought into existence, its role within a wider organisation and the perspective with which it views the wider environment and with which the environment views it.

In industry, teams tend to be 'developed' rather than 'chosen'. If we consider, say, a sporting team (football, cricket etc.) then we often see a team selected by its leader's choice, i.e. Botham may be in the team for this game against this opponent, but not in the next game against other opponents. This relies on there being a 'pool' of virtually idle resources available. In industry there is not, and should not be, a pool of idle resources. Generally, all people already have a function. Teams are usually therefore 'in existence' in some form, and the team leader's job is to focus that existing team and to develop the characteristics of its members to the team's overall advantage. Occasionally there is virgin territory; a new site for a large company which will be able to select its teams from the company's several existing sites world-wide, but even then there are many factors to be considered – individual preferences, promotion and relocation rights, and so on – and in any case there will still be limited numbers to choose from.

Teambuilding is therefore about the development of individuals rather than the selection of them. This has not been appreciated until recently and we must look briefly at the history of teambuilding over the past few decades to see how our present position arises.

All post Second World War teambuilding books, in other words those written during the period when corporate structure has been most deeply psychoanalysed, and perhaps starting with the analysis by Kenneth D. Benne and Paul Sheats in 1948, have attempted to define the team member roles. These analyses have been useful building blocks for teams and teambuilding; indeed we have used these studies in our own work and we happily admit that they are a foundation on which our own studies have been made. Those earlier excellent studies are still valid, but they are based on *psychological* traits, whereas our own categories have focused on communication and influencing skills. They are arrived at in practice, evolving from our work with teams in major companies and – a simple point – we believe the titles to be more clear and descriptive than many that have gone before. However, we have recognised certain changes in the patterns over the years that we have incorporated into our work; probably the most clear are changes in personnel departments which have had something of a 'dehumanising' effect and resulted in the creation of the role that we call the Confessor. In fact, many of the roles detailed in the past have altered to some degree and we have listed below the names we have applied in our training.

It must be said that there has, in our view, been an unnecessary and unhelpful 'blurring' of the definitions between team roles and individual personality types, appointing certain personalities to certain functions. The complexity of team dynamics requires that these definitions be separated and our own practical application for teambuilding in modern organisations has been to isolate the *functions* from the typical *personality types*. The conventional wisdom of teambuilding for many years has been, first, to assume that certain roles are better undertaken by certain individuals and then virtually apologise for the fact that in practical application it can be seen that individuals fail to perform as expected or required in certain circumstances, yet perform adequately in others, depending on a host of environmental criteria. Actually, this apology reflects the fact that the original assumptions are not as valid as previously supposed. The truth is that certain functions must be completed for the team to be effective and the people who perform these roles will be different according to the team, its situation and their own levels of knowledge, hierarchy and so on. The function of the group, with the leader as facilitator, is, in effect, to match the personalities to the functions. The first point to remember is that you cannot apply the personality traits to individual human beings, i.e. you cannot say that, for example, Brian Green is a natural 'harmoniser', that Maria White is a natural 'encourager' or that Charles Brown is always an 'aggressor'. In fact, Mr Green may well be a harmoniser in one particular group situation, but may become an aggressor in another and so on. In fact, even this is over-simplifying the reality; all humans exhibit most of the main personality traits to some degree and if we imagine a graph with different personality traits along the x-axis and a scale of one to ten up the y-axis, then the precise position of each individual trait from one to ten for any individual will reflect the various environmental factors involving that team in that particular situation.

In our experience, therefore, it is vitally important clinically to separate and identify the functions that the team requires to be completed from any human personalities as far as is possible and the team leader's role is then to identify which people in which given situations exhibit the particular balance of characteristics needed to take on the particular roles in question. This is always a dynamic situation; it will depend on the team mission, on whether the team is a long-term structure or a quick response team, on the degree of ownership of the project perceived by the individual team members (which will always be to some degree variable), which in turn will affect the individual energies of the people concerned.

Let us look, then, at these functions which require to be carried out, trying as hard as possible to remove from these definitions reliance on human characteristics. The types of personalities that often appear in these roles are then listed, though not as definitive criteria.

We have divided the required roles into ten, defined as follows.

Visionary

There should be one or more people in the team able to see beyond the team's own requirements. They must have the overall vision of the team mission, as well as a perspective of where that mission fits into the wider organisational objectives. Inevitably, as the name implies, the visionary may not always have his feet firmly 'on the ground'. Part of this function is to 'soar above the clouds' and 'reach for the stars'. There are others whose function is to bring such visionaries back to earth and it is the balance between the two which is the practical and creative force within the team.

Typical characteristics of visionaries include the following.

- They use a 'pull style' of influence, i.e. *pulling* people along by their consent rather than *pushing* them by coercion.
- They are positively optimistic (which is itself a reflection of a pull style of influence.)
- They express openness in an assertive manner, thereby recognising the rights and needs of all parties.
- They are disinterested in detail in this role; preferring the bigger picture (blue skies – no clouds on the horizon!), rather than the components.
- They express impatience, which is also reflected in a need to get on with the big picture rather than tinker about with what they regard as pointless detail.
- They are often frustrated leaders. If there is a team leader then a 'natural' leader will need to find an alternative role and that alternative role will often become that of the team's visionary.
- They don't get a lot done, but then they don't need to because others do all the work while they interpret that vision for them.
- They will often have artistic tendencies.

Pragmatist

It is the pragmatist who acts as foil to the visionary and his or her supporters. At one level the pragmatist identifies the clouds in the visionary's clear blue skies, for example when the visionary has suggested a particular solution to a problem it is usually the pragmatist who reminds the team of budget constraints, or other such practicalities.

At another level pragmatists have a slightly different function. Pragmatists show the team how to make the impossible possible. While, in our above example, it may be their role to remind the visionary of budget constraints, it is also their role to suggest an alternative, building on the visionary's ideas within budget constraints or encouraging other contributions gradually to build up towards a practical suggestion.

Here is a marvellous example of visionary and pragmatist working together; the TV astronomer Patrick Moore tells the story of working for a think tank (i.e. brain-storming body) during the Second World War. He had the undoubtedly visionary idea of constructing a life-size raft of the UK and floating it in the North Sea as a way of confusing German night-time bombing raids. Clearly, it must have been a pragmatist who pointed out that it would require the defoliation of Scandinavia to achieve this result, that it was in any case probably a physical impossibility and of dubious probable success, certainly over the long term. However, there appear to have been alternative pragmatic suggestions building on the visionary's vision and apparently a certain pattern of ships was floated in the North Sea transmitting a particular pattern of signals which would be reminiscent of the signals from the mainland and possibly achieve the result required to some limited degree. The impossible had been made possible.

In the business world perhaps the best example is the contrast exhibited between Sir Clive Sinclair and Alan Sugar, of Amstrad. Sir Clive Sinclair is clearly a visionary, a man whose undoubted genius has created many of the microelectronic marvels which are now taken for granted. However, Sir Clive Sinclair exhibited a limited capacity for producing, marketing and selling his products and it was Alan Sugar of Amstrad who made the impossible possible and built on Sir Clive Sinclair's visions, utilising his genius at the practical level and manufacturing, marketing and selling home computers and so on in the mass market, opening up personal computing as never before. There is perhaps no more pragmatic a statement than Alan Sugar's 'We make money', perhaps the most direct and simple corporate objective ever voiced.

Typical characteristics of pragmatists will include the following.

- They are realistic.
- They favour a push style of influence which is acceptable in the short term, but since it does not enlighten members of the team it is unlikely to succeed in the long term.
- Pragmatists are team players, putting the team before the individual.
- They are disillusioned visionaries and can be summed up in the expression 'I've heard it all before'.
- They tend towards cynicism and scepticism.
- They will often come from a scientific or mathematical background.

Explorer

There will be many times when the team has requirements that it does not automatically fulfil from within. It is the explorer's role to seek information, material, support and so on from outside the team environment. The explorers will build bridges between the team and other teams, or the wider business environment. More than anyone they will form relationships that go beyond the inter-personal relationships of the team itself. They are explorers only from the point of view of the team looking towards its own requirements; they are also ambassadors of the team when the team needs to project beyond itself. This role is not totally new, but has considerably wider application than in the past because of the proliferation of teams resulting from modern corporate methodology. In particular, the upsurge of short-life, quick-response teams mean that explorers need to be highly developed to seek and find resources and information quickly.

Typical characteristics of explorers include the following.

- Sociable, gregarious and forming friendships easily. These are of course necessary in forming the relationships in the world beyond the team.
- Sense of adventure and curiosity. Explorers are not content with the world within the team but need to look into the world beyond.

43

- Competitive.
- Self-starters and self-achievers. Explorers need little motivation from others and are more capable of driving themselves than anyone else is of driving them.
- They are self-made and probably not from an academic background.
- They are good communicators and this provides information flow at the technical level and provides friendships and connections at the social level.

Challenger

There will always be somebody who challenges the accepted position. This may be as little as agreed definitions; the challenger may occasionally request that the team review its own definitions of objectives, progress and so on. It may be as big as challenging even the team mission itself, asking team members to remind themselves of what the mission of the team is, whether it is still relevant after a period of time and so on.

The challenger will also challenge suggestions or proposals made by team members, a further foil to the interaction between visionary and pragmatist. At the worst level the challenger could include such negative individual roles as blocker and nitpicker, but generally speaking the role of challenger is a positive one, as all team roles should be; the challenge is there in order that the team goals are furthered and that the team mission is being fulfilled rather than delayed or distracted.

Typical characteristics of challengers include the following.

- They tend to be defeated visionaries; disillusioned leaders who have seen their own ideals fail.
- They can be prone to cynicism though remaining optimistic (unlike the pragmatist who tends towards scepticism.)
- They will be generalists rather than specialists, but are able to challenge other team members at every level.
- They are extremely curious.
- They will tend to be mavericks or have a rebellious nature.
- They will tend to have business or other failures in their background, but will have learned lessons from these.

Referee

The referee is that person who takes as near an independent view of team progress, decisions and so on as is possible. Clearly as a team member his or her view can never be completely independent and of course there is some blurring at the edges in some teams between referee and challenger, at least in practical approach, i.e. the independent view will usually lead to challenging questions being asked in order that the team evaluate itself from time to time.

However, we believe the roles can be separated for certain team situations on one very important criterion. Challengers are always team members in the sense of being 'company employees', i.e. coming from within the company and being a product of the company culture. Referees, on the other hand, can be outsiders, usually consultants brought in to act as *agents provocateurs* to energise the team, where perhaps it is losing sight of its mission statement. One of the principal roles of management consultants is to challenge on the basis of coming from outside, of not being from the company culture but of looking at the company culture from an even wider perspective, i.e. the overall business environment and the world at large. It is this independence from the company culture which inspires the name referee, since clearly they are not 'team players' in the strict sense of the word, although – to extend the football analogy probably to its limits – they are none the less on the playing field with the teams and have a vested interest in the outcome of the game, albeit not a partisan one.

Typical characteristics of referees will tend to include the following.

- Flexible in style and approach (they have to be able to role-play).
- Neutral, not taking sides and usually able to see both sides of any argument.
- Optimistic and enthusiastic.
- Decisive.
- Daring and courageous.
- Demonstrating a commitment to people and to the task in hand.

45

- Will tend to have a sense of humour.
- Have a reputation for authenticity ('street cred').

Peacemaker

The team will have friction between its individual members from time to time and the peacemaker is the one who will seek to see fair play is done, to try to redress perceived injustices, to harmonise between conflicting views and so on. Previous group role analyses have produced such expressions as 'harmoniser' (i.e. Benne and Sheats), but we have always felt that this implied a certain negativeness, i.e. a repairing function, rectifying damage being done to the team's energies. We have chosen the name 'peacemaker' to imply the positive side that we see in the role, i.e. that part of the job is to predict areas of conflict and head them off before they arise. Perhaps this role is also that of trouble-shooter; this is probably the time to remind ourselves that during the pioneer days in America the most famous Smith & Weston gun was also known as the Peacemaker!

Typical characteristics of peacemakers will include the following.

- They will be good communicators.
- They will be 'people oriented' but not 'task oriented'.
- They tend to have an assertive character.
- They are able to be objective about most matters.
- They have a logical mind.
- They will not allow themselves to demonstrate commitment.
- There will be a strength of character based on an inner belief in self.

Beaver

There is little to be said about the beaver except what is implied by the name, i.e. this is the person who does all the work! The beaver is the worker bee, the soldier ant or more directly the company worker, the Mr/Ms Fix It, etc.

Typical characteristics of beavers will include the following.

- 'Task oriented' rather than 'people oriented'.
- Needing recognition, usually through the achievement of tasks in hand.
- Bedrock, salt of the earth, not creative in their work environment, a typically honest character.
- Will tend to confuse efficiency with effectiveness (concentrating on doing things right rather than doing the right things).
- Will be obsessed with rules and regulations (if Leonardo da Vinci was a visionary then this individual will tend to paint by numbers!)
- Can be oppressively negative.
- Will usually tend to be creative outside the work environment, but rarely inside.
- Not competitive.
- Needs to work in groups and teams in order to feel any sense of achievement.

Coach

Morale is not always going to be high in a team, even in the best-led groups, and there will be times when the team loses its direction or loses its own focus of its mission. It is the coach who is there to boost morale, to shout 'Attaboy!' when the need arises and to remind people of why we are here and what the game plan is, hence the analogy to a sporting coach. This is one of the driving force functions within a team, shouting 'Come on lads!' when the need arises or 'Well done!' at other times.

Typical characteristics of coaches will include the following.

- Tactician and the interpreter of the corporate or team vision.
- Retired visionary (i.e. once was a successful champion – in the golf world Arnold Palmer, once a world champion and now a grand old man of golf, would fulfil this title role).
- Has 'street cred'.
- Will tend to have a mature personality and indeed will often be an older person.
- Has a depth of experience, probably several jobs and will tend to be well travelled.

- Coach is not a role that develops but tends to be an adopted one: they need the flexibility to adopt what can be an unenviable position.
- They are often not concerned with personal popularity. In the army, sergeant majors tend to adopt the role of coaches and will often argue that they can measure their strength in direct relation to the amount of people who dislike them.
- Coaches' visions are quite simply that the team must win at all costs. Once winners, now they believe they must be winners again in this new role.
- Will tend to be teachers.

Librarian

There is an important requirement for someone to be recording, for posterity, the activities of the team. This can include its deliberations, decisions, actions, evaluations and so on. The librarian is the repository to which team members can go for historical information about what the team has been doing, but as the name implies it is also a role with the responsibility for being the depository for information available to the team which may be such information as collected by the explorer etc. Librarians house the information bank from which the others may draw. To use a science fiction analogy, they are the team's 'Mr Spock', though there is no requirement that they should have pointed ears or green skin!

Typical characteristics of librarians tend to include the following.

- They are normally reticent, not interested in small talk.
- Their sense of detail is probably almost out of control; they will be structurists, everything having to be organised and nothing being left to chance.
- Hardworking and diligent.
- Commitment to the team ideals.
- Intolerant and excitable.
- They have crusader instincts developed only through practical research and not through vision.
- They will be good interpreters of facts.

- They tend to be anachronisms, even in their own circle of friends.

Confessor

Team dynamics invariably means that there is a need for someone to whom members can tell all their troubles, a shoulder to cry on, a priest to whom to confess. This is probably the least recognised role and yet practical teambuilding has shown that it is a much valued role. The important requirement of the confessor is of course that stories confided to him or her, i.e. confessions received, remain confidential.

If such a role is successfully established within the team then a great many difficulties can be headed off, but if the person adopting the role should turn out to be little other than a gossip acting as a clearing house for tales and spreading them around then the function is badly negated and, indeed, the team becomes very disharmonious. There is a tendency for this role to fail to arise in teams because it is a role which might naturally fall, on a functional basis, to the team leader and yet by the same token the team leader may well not be the person in whom others wish to confide. If the team leader can encourage the team into finding that role within another member of the group then it takes a great weight from the team leader's shoulders and removes a greater drain on the team's energies.

We consider this to be a new role, since in the past this role did not have significance. With the evolution of personnel departments to human resources strategists now primarily dealing with employment legislation, grading systems and impending legislation such as the 1992 Social Charter, the old personnel department mentality of 'someone whose shoulder is to cry on' has disappeared. The team begins to recognise its own dedicated personnel manager to deal with issues that traditionally would have been dealt with by paid professionals. In our experience of teams we have worked with, this new role seems to be emerging which we have described as the 'Confessor'. Confessors are not experts on legislation or personnel functions, but become a sounding board for the fears and aspirations of the team members who have no other confidant to turn to.

Typical characteristics of confessors will include the following.

- Gregarious and honest.
- Shallow personalities; unable to get too involved and therefore not committed either to tasks or to people.
- They have a low sense of disclosure attracting high disclosure to them from members of the team in the reasonably certain knowledge that they will not pass on confidential information.
- They are normally people of professional status.
- They will tend to be 'in transit'; part of the strength of their position is that they are mobile characters who are not around for the long term and are not able to use or manipulate the information they glean.

We have placed this function last, and particularly beyond that of Librarian, because this is the one repository of information which probably should not be recorded for posterity, whereas the actions of all other functions should be.

It must be stressed here, as it has not yet been successfully stressed in similar books on team characteristics, that these traits are not rigid and amount only to observations from considerable experience. They are particularly able to be identified from personnel records, job applications, CVs etc., but very often surprising 'misfits' – according to our categories – fulfil the most unlikely roles quite successfully. As we stated at the beginning of this chapter, the reason for this is that the roles can be met in a variety of ways and the roles have no real, fixed personality types.

As in so many walks of life, the crisis brings forth the person and the person responds to the crisis.

The team roles questionnaire

Team studies questionnaires designed to indicate personality types are complex and of limited value, given the subtlety of people's predispositions to think and act in a certain way. The following is a questionnaire designed to indicate the particular direction of individual people towards the classifications outlined earlier and will give the team leaders and other team members some indication of their strengths and weaknesses, together with a certain sense of team balance, within their particular groupings.

Each questionnaire is personalised towards one individual who should answer the questions by ringing either 1, 2 or 3, depending on their view of themselves in response to the question. Ringing 3 would indicate either 'I strongly agree' or 'This is very much true of me', 2 would indicate no strong opinion in either direction and 1 would indicate 'This is not very like me' or 'I would strongly disagree with this'. It is recommended that all existing and potential team members complete the questionnaire. Where this is done periodically changes in attitudes will then become apparent.

It is strongly recommended that these questions are answered before looking at the descriptions of the roles in the answer grid at the end of the questionnaire; likewise when this questionnaire is being used for teambuilding exercises the descriptions of the role types should be omitted until the questions have been answered. This will avoid the tendency to inadvertently answer the questions towards a preferred role.

Here are the questions.

1. I feel easy with people.   1 (2) 3

2. Overlooking details is wasteful and dangerous.   1 2 (3)

3. Training others is an investment for the future.   1 2 (3)

4. People can always be replaced, they are not a scarce resource.   1 (2) 3

5. All problems can be broken down into manageable tasks.   1 (2) 3

6. I believe sometimes you have to 'go it alone'.   1 2 (3)

7. I believe that you must take care of details; they cannot be ignored.   1 2 (3)

8. I do not need others to motivate me.   (1) 2 3

9. Many people put forward unworkable or worthless suggestions.   1 (2) 3

10. I see the wider issues; the details don't interest me.   1 (2) 3

11. Companies have become impersonal.   1 2 (3)

12. If you record everything, others can learn by your mistakes.　　1 **(2)** 3

13. I enjoyed a busy life once, now I just want a peaceful one.　　1 **(2)** 3

14. I am active outside work (e.g. gardening, sports etc.).　　1 **(2)** 3

15. I can work with a range of people of varying experience and authority.　　1 2 **(3)**

16. People matter more than things.　　1 2 **(3)**

17. My judgement is usually good.　　1 2 **(3)**

18. Most of what I learnt, that I feel was valuable, was learnt by experience, not by teaching.　　1 2 **(3)**

19. I take the lead when I have to.　　1 2 **(3)**

20. I see how to make connections others don't appreciate.　　1 **(2)** 3

21. I find long conversations with people generally boring.　　**(1)** 2 3

22. The more information you have, the better equipped you are.　　1 2 **(3)**

23. I don't believe people have to like me to do what I ask.　　1 **(2)** 3

24. I expect to be rewarded for work well done.　　1 2 **(3)**

25. I believe spreading gossip causes trouble.　　1 2 **(3)**

26. I do things my way.　　1 2 **(3)**

27. I have had failures; but they have taught me something.　　1 **(2)** 3

28. I like outdoor activities.　　1 **(2)** 3

29. I do not reject ideas just because they seem unworkable; I think them through.　　1 **(2)** 3

30. I am generally optimistic.　　1 **(2)** 3

31. You have to be happy with your work to do it well.　　1 2 ③

32. People find it hard to talk to me about personal things.　　① 2 3

33. Travelling overseas broadens the mind.　　1 2 ③

34. If I have a goal, I strive to meet it.　　1 ② 3

35. People are the most important resource of a company.　　1 ② 3

36. I seek agreement in teams.　　1 2 ③

37. I like to have many alternatives before I make up my mind.　　1 2 ③

38. I believe it's who you know, not what you know.　　1 2 ③

39. I am cautious.　　1 ② 3

40. I am impatient.　　① 2 ③

41. If people are worried about something they cannot work well.　　1 2 ③

42. I am quiet in company, preferring others to do the talking.　　1 ② 3

43. I feel comfortable to be part of a team.　　1 ② 3

44. New ideas are often unworkable.　　1 ② 3

45. I think the team is important to my work.　　1 2 ③

46. I prefer light-heartedness to seriousness.　　1 2 ③

47. I think a broad range of knowledge rather than a depth of knowledge is important.　　1 2 ③

48. I keep up with innovations.　　1 ② 3

49. The team is more important than its individual members.　　1 ② 3

50. I enjoy thinking through complex puzzles.　　① 2 3

51. I believe that honesty is the best policy.　　1 2 ③

52. I take time to make my mind up, but I usually get it right.   1 2 ③

53. Winning is the object of all competition.   1 ② 3

54. If the overall task is explained to me I can plan the way forward, step by step.   1 2 ③

55. I do not often find myself in argument with others.   ① 2 3

56. I believe each problem must be approached on its own merits.   1 2 ③

57. I make up my own rules.   1 ② 3

58. I excite others with my ideas.   1 2 ③

59. I believe people function best if they are given clear instructions and orders.   1 ② 3

60. Others sometimes find me absent-minded.   1 ② 3

61. I enjoy a quiet night at home or a quiet evening socially.   1 2 ③

62. The team vision is important to the company.   1 ② 3

63. The overall vision of the team is very important.   1 2 ③

64. I leave airy-fairy thinking to others.   1 ② 3

65. All ideas have merit, though they may have to be worked on.   1 2 ③

66. There comes a point when you have to make a decision, even if all the facts are not in.   1 2 ③

67. I believe that if you want to get something different out of a situation, you have to put something different into it.   1 2 ③

68. I can draw on a lot of specialist experts with whom I have associations.   ① 2 3

69. I recognise the complexity in problems.   1 ② 3

70. Sometimes my ideas solve long-standing or seemingly insoluble problems.   ① 2 3

71. Formal education and qualifications are important.   1 ②③

72. I don't mind being thought of as a little 'old fashioned'.   ①②③

73. I examine the detail of problems.   1 ②3

74. Rules are made for everyone's benefit; they should be complied with.   1②3

75. I find people seek to confide in me.   1 ②③

76. When I have a task to do, I address myself fully to it.   1 2③

77. I have a high level of curiosity.   1 2③

78. I am excited by new ideas.   1 2③

79. I take time to make up my mind.   1 2③

80. I won't get the best out of others if they don't believe in what I ask them to do.   1 2③

81. I work to live, I don't live to work.   1②③

82. A logical approach is the right way forward.   1②3

83. I believe in being straight with people.   1 2③

84. I like working with others.   1 2③

85. I like to get to know people better.   1 2③

86. I don't believe in kidding people along.   1②③

87. Truthfulness and honesty between people is important.   1 2③

88. I believe a wide association outside the team is vital to my information flow.   1 2③

89. I see pitfalls as they approach.   1②3

90. I often come up with original or radical ideas.   ①2 3

91. I don't see my present position as permanent.   ①2 3

92. I don't suffer fools gladly.   1 2③

93. The whole team must be in consensus about its objectives.   1 2 (3)

94. I believe in an honest day's work for an honest day's pay.   1 (2) 3

95. I do not often feel under stress.   (1) 2 3

96. I believe people must be forced to face problems.   1 (2) 3

97. I think it's good that the team reassesses itself every now and again.   1 2 (3)

98. I examine ideas that might be useful in the future, even though they have no obvious use at the moment.   1 2 (3)

99. I pull the team back on track if it wanders.   1 (2) 3

100. I enjoy 'lateral thinking' exercises.   (1) 2 3

101. A sense of friendliness is important to the smooth running of the team. 1 2 (3)

102. I prefer never to cut corners.   1 (2) 3

103. I like work that stretches the mind.   1 2 (3)

104. I don't like confrontation.   1 2 (3)

105. People who shout the loudest are not always the ones with the right answers. 1 2 (3)

106. I do not always agree with team decisions.   1 (2) 3

107. I believe the team must restate its purposes periodically.   1 2 (3)

108. I do not feel I have achieved all I will achieve in my career.   1 2 3

109. I like to be a key man in group decisions.   1 2 3

110. I believe in thinking independently.   1 2 3

111. I don't betray other people's confidences.   1 2 3

112. The secretary has a vital role to play at team meetings.   1 (2) 3

113. I see mistakes others miss.   1 (2) 3

114. I believe in a systematic approach.   1 (2) 3

115. You learn the most by listening to others.   1 2 (3)

116. Nothing is 'cemented in stone'.   1 2 (3)

117. I am critical by nature.   1 2 (3)

118. I have a wide circle of friends.   1 (2) 3

119. I believe in putting my views forward at team
     meetings.   1 (2) 3

120. I believe people must be open with one another.   1 2 (3)

121. People who shout are generally afraid of
     something.   1 (2) 3

122. I do not find it easy to get on with people.   (1) 2 3

123. People sometimes lose their enthusiasm; if it can
     be reactivated they become energetic people
     again.   1 (2) 3

124. If a job is not clearly defined I have trouble
     knowing what to do.   1 (2) 3

125. I think you have to say what needs to be said; no
     shirking from the facts.   1 (2) 3

126. I am enthusiastic.   1 2 (3)

127. I find arguments that 'kill off' any suggestions.   (1) 2 3

128. I like 'playing with' new technologies.   1 (2) 3

129. I often think out valid alternatives.   1 (2) 3

130. My ideas are not always practical.   (1) 2 3

131. Most people mean well.   1 2 (3)

132. I do not let my feelings affect my work.   1 (2) 3

133. Experience of many jobs is useful; it gives you a
     breadth of knowledge.   1 2 (3)

134. I like to see a job through to the end.   1 2 (3)

135. I stand my ground if I think I am right. 1 (2) 3

136. There is always merit in any point of view. 1 2 (3)

137. I do not let my emotions affect my decisions. 1 (2) 3

138. I keep a broad range of contacts. 1 (2) 3

139. I am a forceful character. 1 2 (3)

140. Very often I find a group constrains my actions; it cannot always put my ideas into practice. (1) 2 3

141. I don't take my work home with me. (1) 2 3

142. Rules make things work. 1 (2) 3

143. I hate to be bored. 1 2 (3)

144. Difficulties are challenges to be met. 1 (2) 3

145. I believe that everyone has a right to an opinion. 1 2 (3)

146. Every problem has a solution. 1 (2) 3

147. I examine ideas in detail. 1 (2) 3

148. I enjoy competitive sports. 1 (2) 3

149. I don't court popularity in the group. (1) 2 3

150. I see problems before they are apparent to others. 1 (2) 3

There are many overlaps between the questions which are designed to approach particular attitudes from several angles. Generally speaking the systematic analysis of results of these questionnaires has given reasonably accurate indications of the types of roles occurring within the teams. From the team leader's point of view the point is not merely to recognise the role but to recognise the strongest traits and develop them according to the best team balance and the needs of the individual. The analysis is done in grid formation on the following outline.

The highest score will indicate a tendency towards that particular role, but of more relevance is the highest cluster around particular ranges of types, for example it would be expected that anyone

Confessor	Librarian	Coach	Beaver	Peacemaker	Referee	Challenger	Explorer	Pragmatist	Visionary
1 3	2 3	3 3	4 2	5 3	6 3	7 2	8 1	9 1	10 1
11 2	12 2	13 3	14 3	15 3	16 3	17 3	18 2	19 3	20 1
21 2	22 3	23 2	24 3	25 3	26 2	27 3	28 3	29 2	30 3
31 3	32 1	33 3	34 3	35 3	36 3	37 3	38 1	39 2	40 2
41 3	42 1	43 3	44 2	45 3	46 3	47 3	48 3	49 3	50 1
51 3	52 3	53 3	54 3	55 2	56 3	57 2	58 2	59 2	60 1
61 3	62 2	63 3	64 1	65 2	66 3	67 3	68 1	69 1	70 3
71 2	72 1	73 2	74 2	75 3	76 3	77 3	78 3	79 3	80 3
81 2	82 2	83 3	84 3	85 1	86 2	87 2	88 2	89 2	90 1
91 2	92 2	93 3	94 3	95 2	96 2	97 2	98 3	99 2	100 1
101 3	102 2	103 3	104 3	105 2	106 3	107 3	108 3	109 3	110 3
111 3	112 2	113 1	114 2	115 3	116 3	117 3	118 2	119 2	120 3
121 2	122 1	123 2	124 2	125 2	126 3	127 1	128 2	129 2	130 1
131 3	132 2	133 3	134 3	135 2	136 3	137 2	138 2	139 3	140 1
141 1	142 2	143 3	144 2	145 3	146 2	147 2	148 2	149 1	150 2
37	29	40	37	38	40	38	32	32	25

showing a high result on Peacemaker might also show relatively high results on Referee, Challenger and perhaps Coach.

It cannot be stressed enough, however, that people are not machines to be turned on to this function or that function; it is far more likely in practice that what mostly happens is that people fall into available roles and therefore if no, say, Confessor role turns up then the 'vacancy' is filled by somebody adopting that role. These questionnaires enable the team leader to discover whether the person adopting the role is best suited to it; and to what extent that person can be supported by training or development in that role.

It is often difficult for individuals to assess the significance of these results; from experience we have learnt that the more often you undertake this exercise the more relevant and understandable the results become. For this reason we strongly recommend that after filling in the questionnaire you discuss the results with your fellow team members.

Where particular roles are absent there is a tendency for the team leader to adopt them him or herself and therefore the more roles absent from the team the harder work the team will be for the team leader. It is therefore in the team leader's interests to import people to the team, where possible, who fulfil certain roles or at least show a tendency towards them in order to produce the required balance for the team.

3. THE TEAM LEADER

'I must follow the people. Am I not their leader?'
Benjamin Disraeli

Probably the greatest influence upon the team is the team leader
and the role played by the team leader./For this reason, since
history was recorded our species has been searching for a set of
universals that will identify what makes a leader, and throughout
history we have seen crude attempts to create a situation or a
world that will grow and nurture future leaders. From the Greek
Academy, to the English public school system, from West Point
to the training in our business schools we are still trying to produce an élite that will take on the future governorship of our
institutions and businesses.

What then makes a Hannibal that thousands of men will follow
over the Alps, what leadership qualities did Napoleon have that
grown men cried at his return from exile, and what list of qualities
can we make about Mahatma Ghandi? The reader will readily see
the complexity of the problem in trying to analyse those qualities
that are required of leaders. All too often any debate on this
subject sparks off the normal platitudes of honesty, integrity,
openness, truthfulness, energy, drive, vision etc., but these are
qualities of good people, and busy people, not always of good or
not so good leaders.

If we then mix good qualities with a skill or a profession, we
end up with good skilled people and good professional people.

When Henry Ford was asked who ought to be the boss he
replied, 'Your question is like asking who ought to be the
tenor in the quartet? Obviously the man who can sing

tenor.' This is a very smart comment on functionality, but of no help on leadership traits.

Let us first examine some of the routes to leadership. The easiest route to the top must be birthright. In the UK, which still has a semi-feudal system, many people still become the boss through the power and influence of the family. Some of our most hallowed institutions and businesses are still run along these lines, though in order for these dynastic institutions to survive the leaders themselves may have to be chosen from near relatives as opposed to the firstborn. Even government is not immune to dynasty; in the House of Lords it is direct descendency of the male line that is regarded as sufficient to influence how the country is governed.

The purest form of leadership must be elective, and when choosing our leaders we have the opportunity to decide upon the qualities and traits that are needed for a particular set of circumstances. Having said that, when we look at the different types of prime ministers we have had since the Second World War, the search for some common traits becomes even more difficult. If we include promotion in this category, i.e. election of a few by a few, then obviously in business we promote people whom management feel have the best fit of qualities to continue the system.

The third route to leadership is through power, normally military or fiscal. People with an army or money can lead nations, but history is catalogued with opportunistic would-be leaders who, having taken over the situation, have led their country and people to disaster. We must accept that Hitler or Mussolini had great leadership qualities, but perhaps not the exact qualities that we want or indeed need for our businesses.

What then are the traits of good leadership, and can we find any universals? Professor John Hunt, in his book *Managing People at Work*, says that his research shows that people who get to the top where leadership is vital are:

- of above-average intelligence;
- from middle to upper-class background;
- healthy;
- possessed of high power needs;
- often firstborn or first son.

Professor Hunt also makes the point that many people who get to the top are not good leaders, concluding that there is not a single set of personality traits from which we are able to predict successful leaders, or conversely from which we can predict non-leaders.

From our empirical observation we can consider some elements of leadership. First, let us look at charisma. Some people are endowed with charisma, this quality of being able to attract people towards them. Charismatic leaders find themselves in very strong positions. John F. Kennedy was certainly a charismatic leader, yet so was Hitler, as witnessed by the extraordinary influence he could exert over mass audiences, in one case standing quietly still for up to five minutes simply allowing people to absorb his presence before he spoke, yet never for a second being denied total attention. However, modern biographers of both leaders have suggested that their charisma was something they could turn on or off at will, and must therefore be a neutral trait. Certainly we cannot tell whether a charismatic leader will turn out to be good or bad.

Secondly, let us look at *gravitas*, or the Roman concept that the chair, i.e. the office, is more important than the person in it and that the office 'grants' power to the office-holder, irrespective of his personal qualities. Without going as far as the Emperor Caligula who threatened to make his horse, Incitatus, a chief magistrate, we can see that certain positions of power do not always require leaders with leadership qualities. Hence the idea, which may or may not be true, that the job maketh the man. In business there are any number of positions of *gravitas*. The new factory manager or the new divisional director may have many or few readily accepted leadership traits, but once in the job he or she assumes all the mantle of power that historically goes with the job.

When Richard Nixon resigned the presidency of the USA, arguably the most powerful job in the world, he stated that he did so to preserve the integrity and the position of the presidency, i.e. its *gravitas*, and to some extent his resignation was due to one of his leadership qualities, that of supporting his aides knowing that they had done wrong.

Most leaders have charisma or *gravitas*, and where the two qualities are combined, or where a charismatic leader gets elected or takes a high *gravitas* position, then you have an unbeatable combination. In these circumstances, as society has found out, people can only hope that the leader has good traits or at least that the good traits outweigh the bad ones.

In John Adair's book, *Effective Leadership*, he makes the point that the leader must look after the task needs of the team, the maintenance needs of the team and the individual needs of the team members. Therefore, to his mind the team leader must give equal consideration to making sure the task is attainable and completed within the specified time; as well as keeping the team together and up to scratch through training and teambuilding, motivation etc.; as well as looking after the individual through recognition and praise, and allowing the individual to grow and develop. These, however, are not leadership qualities, but rather job qualities; more a function of the team leader's role to grow and develop the team for the organisation.

Let us consider the modern business environment which is no doubt more chaotic and difficult to manage now than at any time in this century. Thirty to forty years ago businesses were operating in a more stable environment and the manager, the team leader, could manage in the traditional manner. But are these traditional traits of any use in the new environment? Surely the modern team leader needs a much wider base of skills and the ability to be flexible, than his or her traditional predecessor. Are our institutions producing a new type of leader who can manage in a new way? What are the skills needed from the new leader to lead the new team? In H. Mintzberg's study, *The Nature of Managerial Work*, he identified ten managerial roles which we can apply to the modern team leader. Based on our own observations, our interpretation of those roles is as follows.

- The team leader is a figurehead, representing the team both in the organisation and outwardly to customers, suppliers and other organisations.

- The team leader is a motivator, a coach to the team, installing morale, and identifying and working on the natural motivation flow of the group and of the individuals within the group.

- The team leader is the liaison officer for the team, with outside contacts. Obviously in some circumstances it is possible for the team to meet and work with outside contacts, particularly where a partnership between a company and, say, suppliers have been forged. However, with the time restraints the team leader has to represent the team and interpret the team's needs.

- The team leader is a monitor of information technology (IT). Communication flows are getting increasingly more complex and the new team leader has to monitor IT from all other departments, as well as making decisions as to what information to accept on behalf of the team, and what information the team will have to transmit to the outside world. Having monitored the IT, the team leader will have to disseminate such information and communicate to the team members in informal and formal ways.

- The team leader has also to be the spokesperson on behalf of the team. For this reason the team leaders will need sufficient depth of knowledge of the abilities and potentials of the team so that the best interests of the team can be represented to the outside.

- The team leader often has to demonstrate entrepreneurial abilities, to seek and find opportunities for the team, which will of necessity often involve risk taking on behalf of the team.

- The team leader is a disturbance handler, taking corrective action on behalf of the team. This will also include corrective action within the team, and thereby dealing with personal issues that will inevitably crop up.

- The team leader is a resource allocator for the team. Along with the sub-leaders, the leader will have to allocate moneys, people and authorities within the team.

- The team leader will also have to be a negotiator to internal and external contracts. He or she will have to be briefed by and with the team in order to enter into and conclude negotiations successfully on behalf of the team, and the individual team members.

As management trainers over the years one of the most rewarding experiences we have undertaken is the frank and sometimes heated discussions with managers at all levels of an organisation as to what qualities make a good team leader. Along with that follows the question of what skills and instruction we have to give to emerging team leaders. These we can list and to our minds the challenges of our new way of running our businesses can only be met by the identification of and the building upon such qualities, traits and skills in our team leaders.

- **Communicator**   The team leader has to be a good communicator both within and outside the team. Some people are naturally good communicators and this is often a product of how they were raised and what schools they went to, as well as a factor of encouragement to communicate in the family unit. The ability to communicate, however, demands more than just good verbal and non-verbal skills, which can be taught in business. It demands an open and free flow of communications to and from the team leader. All sense of fear of the organisation has to be removed so that the team leader can state his or her views in a way that can challenge the organisation. The team leader must be supported in this way by the same level of communication development being in place across the whole organisation. Management blocking systems must be broken down and structured vertical lines of communication should be replaced with horizontal and networking lines of communications.

- **Consistency**   The team leader must be consistent in his or her dealings within and outside the team. Consistency is not an excuse for stubbornness. Consistency is often the moral code by which the team leader operates, it is the bedrock of transactions with the team, and then becomes the very elements of reputation and respect by which the team leader will be known.

- **Flexibility**   The team leader needs to be flexible to adapt to the ever-changing circumstances that modern business demands. Flexibility means the attribute to resist entrenched positions and to use experience to tackle new challenges, as opposed to using experience as an excuse to do it in the old way, and only paying lip-service to change by some fine-tuning at the edges.

- **Student**   The team leader needs to be a student, always willing to learn new techniques, systems and new working methods. Additionally, there must be a readiness to take on new types of people and new ideas, and to learn with the team as well as being able to teach the team.

- **Coach**   The team leader needs to be a coach to the team. The coach is responsible for the morale, motivation and well-being of the team. The coach defends the team and individual team members against the internal and external forces that hinder the team in the tasks chosen or set. The coach is responsible for installing a sense of pride in the team and maintaining that sense of pride.

Lastly, the team leader has to be a builder, creating and crafting the team. He or she has to rebuild with new entrants and pull down structures within the team that are working against the team needs. We shall be looking at some of these later.

Perhaps the following most easily sums up the identifiable traits of effective team leaders. They:

- create ideas rather than react to them;
- demonstrate interest in people and what effect decisions have on them;
- are proactive rather than reactive towards situations;
- stir up strong emotions in other people;
- tend to be detached from the day-to-day detail of systems and people issues;
- think through new solutions to old problems;
- regularly create new visible issues for debate;
- paint a large picture, i.e. the vision;
- adopt goals and take an active and personal attitude towards them;
- are good communicators;
- are consistent in dealings both within and without the team;
- are flexible and adaptive to change;
- are students, willing to learn;
- are coaches for the team, responsible for morale and motivation;
- are builders;
- are responsible for looking after the task needs, maintenance needs and individual needs of the team members.

Leadership behaviour can be tested using the checklist questionnaire that follows.

In answering the questions the following key is used.

1 = I rarely believe this or act in this manner
2 = I sometimes believe this or act this way
3 = I often believe this or act in this way
4 = I strongly believe this and act accordingly as much as possible.

Questions

1. The function of my team is to win.   1 2 3 4

2. I demonstrate enthusiasm and commitment.   1 2 3 4

3. I empower my team to act as independently as possible within the corporate boundary rules.   1 2 3 4

4. I forgo personal preferences for the benefit of the team.   1 2 3 4

5. I use my expertise and skills for the benefit of the team, as opposed to my own personal gain.   1 2 3 4

6. I communicate the intentions of senior management with openness and honesty.   1 2 3 4

7. Without me the team would not function as effectively as it does.   1 2 3 4

8. I seek recognition and reward on behalf of my team.   1 2 3 4

9. I share success with my team.   1 2 3 4

10. I share set-backs with my team.   1 2 3 4

11. I perceive set-backs as opportunities.   1 2 3 4

12. I socialise with my team.   1 2 3 4

The minimum score is 12; the maximum 48; the average 30.

A score of 12 to 30 would suggest that although you may be a team leader you are not demonstrating the accepted characteristics of that position's required behaviour. You may therefore be holding back the energy and commitment of your team members.

A score of 31 to 47 suggests that you demonstrate your commitment to the team by your behaviour and you are prepared to sacrifice short-term gain for long-term teambuilding.

A score of 48? Who do you think you're kidding? Go back and do it again more honestly!

4.   THE STAGES OF TEAM DEVELOPMENT (READY–STEADY–GO)

'All happy families resemble each other, while each unhappy family is unhappy in its own way.'

Tolstoy, *Anna Karenina*

The above may or may not be fair of families, but it is certainly true of teams. Teams in difficulty offer a wide range of problems, but the successful teams all tend to exhibit similar characteristics: openness; energy; enthusiasm; commitment; and so on.

However, it is perhaps inevitable that teams do not begin functioning effectively from the outset. Teams need a certain time to arrange themselves into an effective force and all teams basically go through three stages, of which the last is their effective stage. We have summed these up with the simple expression **READY–STEADY–GO**.

Ready

This is the period immediately after the team is put together. There will be a tendency for the team to be enthusiastic and energetic, but to lack fully developed interpersonal relationships between team members and to lack certain direction within the company as it begins to flex the muscles given to it by its team contracts. The **READY** stage is one of chaos and confusion with much energy resulting in very little achievement. It is soon recognised that the team lacks a certain order.

Quite often the team assumes that it understands its objectives, and others within the company assume that they understand the company's objectives, but both are often wrong. As we have

70

shown earlier, it is one of the basics of team contracts that assumptions must be replaced by clear statements. There is usually very little time planning as to how to approach team tasks, as there will be no experience of the effectiveness of the team members. Perhaps most importantly there will either be no true leader to the team, or the leader will be unclear as to their authority, or even their role. As a result the **READY** stage can often create ideas without effect because the debating structure within the team is not in existence. Any successes achieved will be reduced.

Soon it becomes recognised that in order for the team to progress it must impose a certain order and then the team is ready to move on to the next stage. . .

Steady

This stage takes its name from the fact that in order to create the structure for the **READY** stage to be progressed, certain formalities are imposed. There will then be a concentration of rules and obeying the rules, unfortunately often at the expense of team objectives. In other words it is perceived that the team is creating and obeying rules for rules' sake, rather than showing the intuition needed to break the rules where necessary. The **STEADY** stage is rigid and over-planned. Strong leadership develops as a foil to earlier uncertainties. It may be at this stage that the team's formal leader is seen not to be a natural leader and indeed there may be some conflict between a natural leader within the group and the person nominated for the position. At this stage there will be a tendency to blame scapegoats, usually on the basis of non-observance of rules. The **STEADY** stage is characterised by the assignment of specific job tasks, formalised job descriptions and constant monitoring of adherence to job descriptions. The stage becomes redundant as the team recognises that it is now spending more of its time obeying the rules than achieving the tasks and gradually it begins to move to the next stage. . .

Go

The **GO** stage, the stage at which the team is most effective, grows out of the **STEADY** stage when there is both a recognition of certain systems and rules while recognising that the task at hand is the main priority rather than the procedures. The **GO** stage is flexible and allows for revised objective settings and plannings. The leader that has emerged at this stage will be a supportive, empowering leader, rather than a directive, controlling leader. Indeed, there are times when the group may say something to the effect of, 'Our leader doesn't seem to be very effective but none the less it's amazing that we get an awful lot done'. This, in fact, is a compliment to the leader who is clearly allowing his or her well-developed team to realise its full potential. The **GO** stage is also characterised by shared responsibility and recognition for successes with the team members recognising and being recognised for their individual and collective contributions. There is an atmosphere of trust and co-operation during this stage between members, between the team and the company, and in the broader environment. In other words the various contractual obligations of the team (see Chapter 1) are being fulfilled. Most importantly, it is only at this stage that the team is successful in achieving its, and the company's, objectives.

Team dynamics are just that – dynamic. If the team exists within the **GO** stage for long enough then there is a degeneration towards the **STEADY** stage, most apparent in increasing formality and the rigid adherence to the rules. A certain entropy will set in. It is training maintenance and team development which can keep the team at the **GO** stage for the longest possible time. However, it is rapidly becoming recognised that very long-term teams are not an adequate reflection of the constant change within which the modern business entity operates. Indeed, it often represents teams which are now functioning for their own sake rather than to meet any objectives at all. Quite often a team will be created, for example, to decide on a set of standards of operating procedures which it will then achieve, but having brought itself into being it then begins to scrabble around examining the most irrelevant and bizarre aspects of company activity, creating standards where they are not necessary, because it exists simply to set standards rather than to meet required objectives. Either the lack of objectives must be recognised and the team disbanded or regenerated (see Chapter 16), or the team's objectives must be restated or redefined to give it a new sense of purpose. Failing to do this can drive a team that was at the **GO** stage back down the ladder through **STEADY** and back to the disorganisation of the **READY** stage.

Different cultural backgrounds can have an influence on team dynamics. We have studied the operations of some Japanese companies and they exhibit differences in decision-making and implementation from their North-west European, or American, counterparts. These differences affect the time the teams spend in each of the **READY–STEADY–GO** stages. In brief, Japanese companies tend to spend longer in the **READY** stage, but move very quickly through the **STEADY** stage and are able to **GO** swiftly. Furthermore, they stay at the **GO** stage for longer, though training maintenance will be a factor here. They may seem to dither for a long time, but they then implement with astonishing speed.

Decision-making in the West is so well known that for many people the existence of an alternative is probably not recognised. Yet this 'Eastern' style of decision-making is quite different, and significantly affects corporate teambuilding and team results.

It has to be admitted that a convenient dividing line is being drawn here where none really exists; it is more a blurred shading of greys. There are companies in the 'West' that apply 'Eastern' principles and vice versa. Furthermore, many companies have operated in both environments and have attracted aspects of both of the systems that are described below. Perhaps more importantly, the division was never really 'West' and 'East', but rather one of cultural background. However, in its earliest days it can be shown that the 'Western' principles below arose very much in America and North-west Europe, where corporate structure was built on military lines, and the Eastern principles are more easily identified in Japanese companies. For the sake of simplicity we shall refer, then, to West and East.

Imagine that we are a team of eight people, and we have to decide between two major, long-term projects which will commit considerable resources for many years to come. We are planning the development of a multi-million pound manufacturing plant, but with a choice of alternative designs and purposes. Let us look at how those differences affect the team dynamics:

WEST	EAST
1. Begin with the facts	Begin with opinions

It may seem obvious to Western-style thinking that you cannot proceed until you have facts; but the Eastern style would look first at opinions, deliberately ignoring facts. The first commitment of the West is to 'facts', whereas the first commitment of the East is to understanding the situation. This means that a lot of time is saved by not collecting wrong facts. Take a non-corporate example which shows the problem well. During the late 1980s and early 1990s, the Conservative government was accused of being out of touch with the needs and wishes of the people. A commitment to facts would have the government seeking to identify the areas where it was out of tune with the people – in this case examining which of its policies were unpopular and also what policies people wanted that were not being offered. However, a commitment to understanding would first have addressed the question, 'Are we sure we are out of touch, or are we simply not presenting our policies effectively?'. The problem may not be policies but PR, yet it would be easy to address the wrong problem if the understanding was missing. That said, there are many who believe that this was the exact mistake the government did make, perhaps losing in Margaret Thatcher a most valuable – but perhaps misunderstood – asset.

WEST	EAST
2. Focus on the answer	Focus on the question

If you think you have the facts then you can search for an answer. In the East the emphasis is on being sure you are trying to answer the right question.

WEST	EAST
3. Pressure for agreement	Wide variety of opinions explored

In our team of eight people, armed with the facts as we see them, or even opinions, there is a struggle between us all in the West to 'make the other person agree' with us. Not so in the East where people are encouraged to disagree far more. This is in fact one of the first principles of brainstorming (creative, lateral thinking) – the East had already been doing it for years before we named it!

WEST	EAST
4. There is a right solution	There are alternatives

There is a strong belief in the West that if enough facts and opinions are studied for long enough, then the solution produced will be the only right one, or at least, perhaps, the best one. This is believed less in the East where it is recognised that any collection of facts will have several solutions; and each is probably equally valid. Each might produce similar results, and the choice is actually more open. Further, in a situation of constant dynamic change in modern business, which is the business environment in which we work, it is actually impossible accurately to predict the outcome of a long-term project of many years. The project undertaken must be capable of flexibility. No chosen solution can be certainly regarded as the 'right' one, probably not even the best. It will be merely the most acceptable in a current climate of equal choices.

WEST	EAST
5. Answers can be proposed at any time	No solutions allowed until there is consensus about the question

Often in the West there is a sense of relief when someone offers a solution; a sense of 'Good, that's that dealt with, now we can get on with something else' (i.e. lunch, game of golf etc.!). This can lead to plumping for quick-fix solutions rather than building long-term structures.

WEST	EAST
6. Facts needed to fit the conclusion already reached	Find out why people disagree

If a quick solution is grabbed out of the air there is then a tendency to seek out facts which fit the solution, to justify the course of action taken. It is more effective, of course, if the solution is designed to fit the facts! This means that there is a need (the Eastern method) to ask the question of dissenting opinion-holders, 'What do these other people see that makes their alternative seem more rational to them?'. Another valuable question is 'What would the facts have to be to make their position correct?'. New facts can be uncovered by this, or often the alternative is seen to be flawed because the facts do not support it.

WEST	EAST
7. The team must stand together	The team now divides

Perhaps the most important part of the process now arises. Let us assume that in our team of eight we have a split of opinions; five want Project A and three want Project B. We might assume that Project A will be chosen (it doesn't have to follow, but it probably would). In the West the five committed to Project A now have to exert pressure on the other three to 'come along with them'. Inducements may be needed, even covert threats to job security. Certainly a great deal of energy is used to 'sell' Project A to the other three. Not so in the East, where implementation of Project A would be done by a team of the five people committed to it; they would then draw in others to assist who felt able to support the project. The other three will go off to do something else. Their energies will be better utilised on a project to which they are fully committed, and if the company has no such projects then they must consider if this is the company for them. On the other hand, Project A now moves forward with great energy; every member of the team is committed to it fully from the word go.

This tends to mean, in practice, that the East takes far longer to decide what to do than the West, but can then do it far quicker. Consider the motor-cycle industry. The British led the world in motor-cycle production and could not see the Japanese coming in their rear-view mirrors; the Japanese seemed to be floundering about in their attempts to break into the market. By the time the British saw them closing the distance on the racetrack behind them, it was too late. The Rising Sun overtook them, roared off into the distance and left the British motor-cycle industry to appreciate the splendours of the Setting Sun.

Practical effect

The West tends to be able to make small, easy decisions quickly, but often cannot make the best decisions for the long term. In the East small decisions often get ignored, but big decisions are well thought out and have longevity even in a changing world of corporate chaos.

Having examined the basics of teambuilding it is appropriate that the reader consider the team(s) in which he or she is currently working.

The following checklist is designed to allow the team members to examine a team's stage of progress; indicating whether it is in the **READY–STEADY–** or **GO** stage.

Compliance is reported on a scale of one to six, with high (positive) compliance at six and low (poor) compliance at one.

1. Our team makes effective use of ideas and contributions.   1 2 3 4 5 6

2. Our team achieves a great deal.   1 2 3 4 5 6

3. The team's 'vision' is clear to all team members.   1 2 3 4 5 6

4. Our team leader's role is well defined.   1 2 3 4 5 6

5. Communication is good in our team.   1 2 3 4 5 6

6. Our team is proactive, not reactive.   1 2 3 4 5 6

7. Implementation of decisions taken by the team is made clear to us all.   1 2 3 4 5 6

8. We plan our actions well.   1 2 3 4 5 6

9. Formality is kept to a minimum.   1 2 3 4 5 6

10. There is collective acceptance of both success and set-back.   1 2 3 4 5 6

11. Our procedures have proven themselves to be effective.   1 2 3 4 5 6

12. The group is self-disciplined.   1 2 3 4 5 6

13. The company supports the team with adequate resources.   1 2 3 4 5 6

14. There is openness and frankness in all team discussions.   1 2 3 4 5 6

15. Our team is equipped with or supported by an adequate skills base.   1 2 3 4 5 6

16. There is a high level of trust between team
    members.   1 2 3 4 5 6

17. The team is able to be effectively flexible
    when the need arises.   1 2 3 4 5 6

18. There is a high level of commitment to the
    tasks and to the individuals.   1 2 3 4 5 6

19. We enjoy our work.   1 2 3 4 5 6

20. Decisions are made by consensus, never by
    imposition.   1 2 3 4 5 6

21. Our learning and training procedures are
    effective.   1 2 3 4 5 6

Results analysis:

A score of 21 to 50. Depending on how long your team has been in existence you are either in the **READY** stage and about to move on, or you are stuck in it. Either way, some reflection is needed. Your team, probably through an unclear vision and communication problems, has insufficient team skills to work together. The team is demonstrating low task and low people skills, a lack of commitment and is in a reactive (rather than proactive) mode. A brainstorming session is recommended to reassess why the team was formed in the first place and what teambuilding games will be necessary to build and unite it.

Should you identify that your team is in the **READY** stage then we recommend the following course of action:

- re-define the objectives of the team and get the team to re-commit to them;
- critically examine the role of the team leader and agree with that person why the team is stuck at **READY**;
- examine the skills base of the team (see Chapter 10);
- introduce some formality into the team, i.e. the setting of agendas, timings etc. without crushing the synergy of the team (see Chapter 15);
- establish the role being played by team members by using the questionnaire set out in Chapter 2.

A score of 51 to 90. Like most mature teams you are in the

STEADY stage, but may be in danger of being too steady and getting stuck. You have discovered enough about yourselves, and worked together long enough, to satisfy corporate and team objectives, but you are not stretching yourselves. Your team knows where it is going, but it needs to go faster. It is now time to get off the corporate fence and re-energise through focusing the team, to enter the **GO** stage.

Should you identify that you are in the **STEADY** stage then we recommend the following:

- re-define the objectives of the team (which may have changed) so that the team can be re-focused and energised (see Chapter 5);
- the team leader should hold a brainstorming session to establish and agree why the team is reliant upon formality at the expense of action, and realise that some encouragement to take risks may be necessary if the team has become too 'comfortable';
- it may, as a last resort, be necessary to tear up the 'rule book' and agree with the team that rules are no longer necessary at this stage in the development.

A score of 91 to 126. Congratulations! Your team is in the **GO** stage, and knows why it is in being and where it is going. Your team is an ideal training ground for new entrants and a good base for developing the individual members of the team, including the team leader. Your team is demonstrating high task and high people skills, it is empowered, and has the support and encouragement of strong management, and reliable corporate systems.

Do remember that it takes effort to maintain a good team, so do not neglect training maintenance.

We have earlier pointed out that teams can 'slide back' from the **GO** stage to the **STEADY** stage, unless there is conscious effort made to maintain the team's energy and focus through a re-definition of objectives, vision etc. The questionnaire should therefore be used periodically to act as a reminder to teams of where apathy might be setting in.

5. ENERGISING AND FOCUSING

'Cheshire puss, would you please tell me which way I ought to go from here?'

'That depends a good deal on where you want to get to,' said the cat.

'I don't much care where,' said Alice.

'Then it doesn't matter which way you go,' said the cat.

'So long as I get somewhere,' Alice added, as an explanation.

'Oh, you're sure to do that,' said the cat, 'if you only walk long enough'.

Lewis Carroll, *Alice's Adventures in Wonderland*

A team cannot be effective unless its energies are united and focused. Throughout the chapters of the book there are examples of ways in which the team will be united by a variety of circumstances and actions. There is, however, no more united a team than one which is focused towards its goals.

Past goals

Traditionally, team focus has been on goals which we now recognise were either too limited or in any case dealt with the symptoms without dealing with the disease. Primary among these goals was probably the vision of profit. Teams would have a stated objective of simply locating ways of increasing profit. Of course, there is nothing wrong with making profit, but if the team is energised only towards that goal – and since all teams are expected to produce tangible results – then there is a tendency to look for short-term profit at the expense of long-term survival or growth. Alternatively, teams might be energised to look for ways of increasing market share, i.e. looking at survival and growth. On that basis short-term profit is easily sacrificed and the company finds much of its fat cut away and is indeed unable to survive any unpredictable changes in the economy in which it is working.

The problem was that these objectives were *conceptual*; having identified a problem energy was given merely to dealing with it and not with the root causes that had allowed it to occur in the first place. What was needed were *behavioural* objectives which would change the attitudes within the corporate structure at its roots. If the conceptual objectives were treating the symptoms, then it is the behavioural objectives which are the prevention that is better than the cure.

The second problem was that the traditional conceptual objectives were often in conflict within the organisation. To give a simple example, if the short-term goal is profit, then the sales force could easily be instructed simply to make as many sales as possible. This they can do by merely offering sales to people who are perhaps less than credit-worthy. The credit control department, however, which may also be under the directive to increase profits, will be told to continue to collect debts efficiently, or indeed to increase efficiency and reduce the outstanding debtor period. They will find it less easy to do if sales have been made to people who are not credit-worthy and for whom proper credit checks have not been undertaken. Since it is likely to be the credit control department that undertakes the credit checks and may therefore prevent the sale in the first place, there are two potential sources of conflict between these two departments; either because sales that are being pushed for by the salesperson will not take place or sales which do take place do not result in income. What are therefore needed are common goals and behavioural objectives which can be applied across the board and throughout the company, but which allow for departmental interpretation within a common structure.

What has emerged in recent years are principally two forms of focus, one of which applies largely to manufacturing, or at least in some way the handling of goods, and one of which applies to service industries.

Total quality management (quality focus)

> 'I see you stand like greyhounds in the slips,
> Straining upon the start. The game's afoot:
> Follow your spirit, and upon this charge
> Cry "God for Harry, England, and Saint George!"'
>
> William Shakespeare, *Henry V*

Before going into battle, the king, at the head of his armies, raises his standard (the origin of the expression) as a sign to all the team members (i.e. the army) of what is expected of them. The king does not address the archers and tell them he wants them to learn to fire their arrows straight or round corners or ricochet them off trees or whatever, and he does not address the pike men and tell them how to thrust or cut; these are merely practical matters. What the king does is to instil behavioural objectives (i.e. you will fight to the death for your king and country). Technical matters such as archery would be left to his departmental managers (i.e. the individual army commanders), but he provides the backdrop against which all other corporate objectives are played. If the army were brilliantly technically skilled, but ran away at the first sight of an enemy, there would be few battles won. On the other hand, an army truly energised to fight to the death because it really believes in king and country and all that that encompasses even in the most clichéd sense, is going to be a formidable fighting weapon, whatever its technical skills. Further, if that determination and energy is applied to all the army, including the commanders, they will see it as part of their duty to train the archers not just to fire the arrows straight, but also to be prepared to continue to do so in the face of murderous hoards bearing down on them. With the behavioural objectives instilled, with the technical skills taught and with the team (i.e. the army) energised and united in its focus, then all it takes is for the king to raise his standard and the army becomes one massive, intricate, co-ordinated fighting machine.

Enough of murder and mayhem for the moment. We must now return to the more cold-blooded battle ground of the board room.

Because it is fairly recent, the introduction of total quality management (TQM), also known as quality focus, or, more simply, quality, has been somewhat misunderstood by companies. The reason it has been misunderstood is because it has been taken to be yet another conceptual goal rather than a behavioural objective. We will take perhaps the most obvious aspect of the TQM, and certainly the most criticised in the large companies where we have worked, that of zero defects. First it has to be understood that there is a certain dichotomy of thinking which has to be accepted, i.e. we truly seek production processes which produce no defects whatsoever, and we truly believe that one day that goal will be achieved while at the same time we hold in our mind the knowledge that such a goal is impossible. It seems at first that the mind cannot hold conflicting concepts, yet in fact even a simple example shows that it does so very well.

Question: 'Does a unicorn have one horn?'
Answer: 'Yes.'
Question: 'Do unicorns exist?'
Answer: 'No.'

In the quality analysis the resolution to this dual thinking comes from understanding that zero defects is not a conceptual goal, rather a behavioural pattern. At that point it becomes apparent that it is the quest for zero defects which is more important than the achievement of such.

Therefore, with TQM there can be a quality focus throughout the whole corporate organisation, i.e. TQM becomes the king's standard and all members of the workforce, such as departmental managers, departmental directors and so on are able to direct their efforts, and the efforts of their subordinates, towards the one common standard. The thinking processes of every individual are therefore directed towards a common goal.

If TQM suffers from any particular defects of its own at the present time, it is probably only communication and lack of training, a failure to explain its behavioural concepts to those at the shopfloor level who have to implement their part of it. The training element is often ignored and although staff have no problems with the concept and common sense of TQM, problems do arise in the lack of formal training in numerate skills for measurement, written communication skills for reports and problem-solving techniques which, in most of our organisations, are becoming computer-based. TQM is therefore not attainable without the up-front investment in training and training maintenance to allow staff to own the process.

Because TQM demands measurable results it is applicable for the most part to production processes where output can be measured in terms of good quality finished products or man-hours spent without injury, and so on. It is less applicable to service industries where the following alternative is applied. However, as a unifying focus for teams within large companies TQM will, in the years to come, prove to be one of the first truly behavioural standards.

Customer focus

For service industries achievement objectives, i.e. success, cannot be measured by looking at the products produced or by health and safety factors. The only true measure of success is customer focus, i.e. is the customer satisfied with my work? The concept is still one of total quality and the standard raised by the king in our earlier analogy still applies. However, in order that the service company knows it is producing quality, it relies on its customers to tell it. The question must not therefore be 'Am I supplying the best service of its kind available?' (which may only be successful because of poor competition), but rather 'Am I supplying what my customer really wants?', 'Does my customer really want what I sell or is he simply accepting it as the best of a bad lot?'.

There is the analogy of the man walking through the streets of a collapsing city during a major earthquake. While the ground is boiling and the buildings are falling down around him, the man offers people on the streets pills for the earthquake. 'Will they do any good?', asks one man. 'Probably not,' replies the vendor, 'but what alternative have you got?'

Customer focus is therefore not a conceptual specific, but rather a behavioural pattern, indeed it is a vision and allows the team a permanent understanding of an overall goal and for interpretation down to the finest level of detail, whether or not the person doing the interpreting is the managing director or the tea-boy.

Who is the customer?

To understand customer focus fully it must be clearly understood precisely who the customer is. A simple definition will suffice to begin with, i.e. the customer is a person who buys goods and services from you. There are some clear-cut examples of customers, for example in a shop the person walking in and buying goods from the shelves and paying for them is the shop's customer. However, the concept of customer has broadened greatly, particularly in large companies where there are many 'internal' customers, and many large companies have service departments who regard other parts of the company as their customers.

For example, in one major company in which we work the training department regards all other departments of the company as its customer, and it views itself as a supplier of services which are bought and sold within the company. In some cases this is taken to its literal extreme where the training department has to be competitive and where the other departments have the right either to use the training department facilities or go outside the company for better facilities elsewhere. This sharpens that department's customer focus very clearly and makes it very important that the internal training department is supplying what is needed rather than what it wants to supply.

Although it is probably not done in smaller companies this system is extremely effective and if the tea-boy in a small company viewed the other staff in the company as his customers who he had to woo against other competition, then presumably the quality of his tea would be that much greater, particularly when consistent buying from his competitors (i.e. nipping down the café and getting half-a-dozen polystyrene containers of tea!) would eventually result in our tea-boy having to nip down to the dole office to collect his unemployment benefit!

Traditionally, the one area where customers are most easily defined is also the area where customer focus is lowest. Shop staff are, often rightly, criticised for being very poor suppliers to customers and indeed having little customer focus. Everyone has had the experience of being served by somebody who never even looks at you, who continues carrying on their conversation with their colleagues while snatching money from you and throwing the products back at you and who, if challenged, would argue 'I don't get paid any more or less whether I am polite or not, it makes no difference to my job'. (A remarkably naïve view considering the number of people at the unemployment benefit office who now have the time to reflect on those words.)

Customer focus becomes, therefore, not a conceptual reaction to customer needs, but rather a behavioural reaction to your own attitudes towards your customers. Again, it becomes a standard which energises and focuses the attention of the team towards the one common goal.

Practical steps in achieving energy and focus

Simplify processes and procedures

If work is made easy then time is released to do other things and appreciate the bigger picture. To take a very simple example, if there were no such things as alphabetical systematic filing, if every piece of paper that needed to be retrieved had to be sought for at random among every other piece of paper available, then a massive amount of time would be spent simply searching for pieces of paper. Apart from increasing the number of staff needed, those staff employed on that task would be demotivated by the boredom of their work and would have very little time for looking up to see the king's standard fluttering in the breeze.

No quick fixes

Many teams find themselves in the position of doing no more than fire fighting, i.e. putting out fires rather than preventing them. Even if they are successful, there is no time to appreciate an overall corporate vision or to extend the company's objectives in new directions. It is also extremely demotivating. Ask any trainers, such as the authors of this book, what the most common complaint from line-managers or departmental managers is and it will be 'All we ever do around here is deal with crises, we hardly ever get time to plan anything'. Planning is essential and action should be permanently effective rather than merely quick fixes which will fall apart at the next potential crisis. 'The best preparation for tomorrow is to do today's work superbly well,' said Sir William Osler.

Empower the team

Empowerment is exciting. It is the process of allowing the team to test the boundaries of its responsibilities and capabilities. Consider Tom Wolfe's book, *The Right Stuff*, where the test pilots were described as 'pushing out the edge of the envelope', i.e. taking their aircraft further and further beyond their known limits. What made their job exciting was not being told where the limits were, but pushing themselves to those limits and beyond to find out exactly where they lay.

Many test pilots died in the course of their work, indeed the mortality rate in the early days of jet-engine testing was extremely high. Eventual success was achieved, though, and here we find a lesson for industry in that failure is not something to be avoided, rather it is a vital component of success.

Rabbi Harold Kushner, author of *When Bad Things Happen to Good People*, states that failure 'teaches you something about your strengths and acquaints you with your limitations'. The team should be encouraged to test its limits, and that can only happen if the team leader and those the team reports to are prepared to accept failure. The business ethic which condemns failure as a bad thing is going to restrict its best people, force them to avoid taking risks that may one day be beneficial and will prevent the team experiencing the excitement of the empowerment which is vital to motivation and team dynamics.

Training

The team must be supplied with the means to learn and develop. As stated above, that development must include encouraging both success and failures. It is worth noting that the Chinese 'word picture' for crisis is a combination of 'danger' and 'opportunity'. The team must be prepared to meet difficulties and failure in order to experience not just how it deals with failure, but also how to turn it into opportunity. Supportive training on a technical basis must also be available to the team in order that it can meet the requirements of its customers and of existing technologies. Team training is discussed in Chapter 10, but should be fully integrated and forward planned to form part of the team's overall behavioural objectives.

Lead by example

The expression 'Do as I say and not as I do' should be one of the few phrases for ever banned from team dynamics. No one should ever ask the team to do something which is contrary to the example that person is setting.

Loyalty

Loyalty must be continuous and explicit so that the team knows its work is being fully supported by the rest of the corporate infrastructure. That loyalty must be unwavering in good times as well as bad. There is the old joke of the Lone Ranger and his Indian friend Tonto cantering through the plains of the Wild West when they suddenly find half a dozen renegade Indians following them. The Lone Ranger asks Tonto, 'What shall we do?' and Tonto replies, 'There is no problem Kimo Sabe, just keep riding on'. Shortly afterwards the duo are followed by a hundred such Indians and the Lone Ranger asks the same question and Tonto replies the same. Eventually they discover they are being pursued by thousands of Indians and the Lone Ranger asks the same question, 'What shall we do now, Tonto?' and Tonto replies, 'What do you mean *we*, paleface?'.

Show the vision

People must be shown the corporate vision and where their own work fits into that vision. They must see and appreciate the input they have. It is not sufficient simply to say, 'You are doing good work', it is important that the person sees, and is told, that they are doing good work in that it is progressing the corporate objective in this way or that way. Similarly, they must have the opportunity of helping to create that corporate vision as described below.

Appreciation of the value of work

Just as people must appreciate the contribution they are making to the company, so their work must be appreciated for its own efforts and its own sake, and the team leaders must make an effort consciously to praise and reward good work.

Ownership of projects

The team must be encouraged to own projects mainly by having a part in designing them. (This is dealt with in more detail in Chapter 6.)

Structured brainstorming session

There are a number of games that teams can play which are useful both in cementing team relationships and also in helping team members to discover creative thinking. These games create energy and focus for the team. Since there is no limitation to the scenarios possible for brainstorming sessions we use many non-business, entertaining games such as the one below.

You are the captain of a spaceship on a mission of exploration. You are 1,000 light years from Earth, in a nebula cloud which is the result of a massive stellar explosion.

You encounter an alien spacecraft.

From your preliminary data you determine that:

- the aliens are very human-like;
- they live in an atmosphere and gravity similar to Earth;
- they have similar fears and emotions to Earth people.

YOU WILL NEED TO CALL ON YOUR ADVISERS BUT AS THE CAPTAIN YOU MUST DECIDE ON A COURSE OF ACTION.

USE FISHBONE ANALYSIS TO DISPLAY THE PROBLEM AND USE BRAINSTORMING TO FIND THE SOLUTION.

The first task the team should apply itself to is to identify whether there is a problem and, if so, what the problem is. Only once that

SUGGESTED FISHBONE:

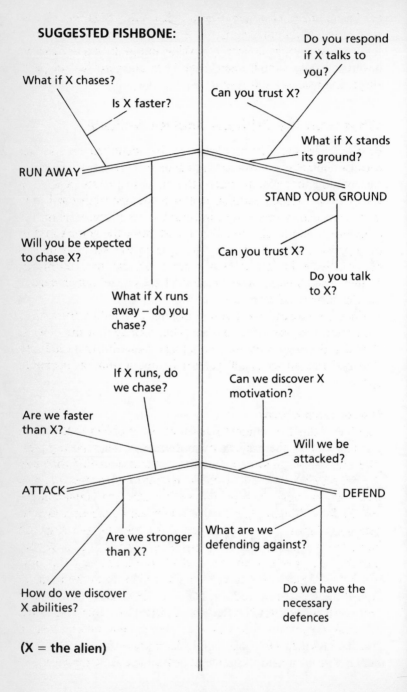

Do you respond
if X talks to
you?

What if X chases?

Is X faster?

Can you trust X?

What if X stands
its ground?

RUN AWAY

STAND YOUR GROUND

Will you be expected
to chase X?

Can you trust X?

Do you talk
to X?

What if X runs
away – do you
chase?

If X runs, do
we chase?

Can we discover X
motivation?

Are we faster
than X?

Will we be
attacked?

ATTACK

DEFEND

Are we stronger
than X?

What are we
defending against?

How do we discover
X abilities?

Do we have the
necessary
defences

(X = the alien)

has been done can the team begin to determine what the solution is. Because of the unusual nature of the problem the team often follows a wide range of lateral thinking and in the many times we have used this example there have been an incredible range of surprising analyses and results.

What does the fishbone analysis indicate?

Broadly speaking the problem can be identified as follows: because the nebula is so fierce it stands to reason that no planet can exist in the area, therefore the alien spacecraft must be a visitor from a remote location just as is the one from Earth. On that basis neither spaceship can return to its planet because the other one would be able to follow it and locate the home world of the opposing race. Both races are able to live on each other's planets. Since the intentions of neither race can be determined, neither spaceship can in fact leave the location without endangering the survival of their race.

Since both races have a vested interest in building trust, then both might be persuaded to 'test' their craft agai.·st the other's. Provided that the results were equal, and assuming that the Earth ship had run up to its full potential, then a solution begins to appear.

One solution offered
The key factor lies in identifying that the problem is that both races know only the minimum capabilities of the opposing race. The solution lies in switching spacecraft and switching therefore the minimum knowledge to the maximum knowledge, i.e. you may not know what the capabilities of the alien spacecraft are, but you do know they are at least capable of reaching the same as your maximum limits. When you have got that race in your ship you know the maximum they are capable of because it is your ship that they are operating and presumably the aliens have the same information. Since you have tested their ship up to the limits of yours, you know that you can now only be equally powerful or more so and presumably they have done the same test. (One practical suggestion that was also pointed out in one session was that it would be highly advisable to erase the memory tapes in the ship's on-board computers which would otherwise give

information about the Earth so that the whole exercise would be a waste of time.)

During the various sessions we have held there have been some very radical solutions and one person suggested that the risk was far too great and that the only solution was to detonate the ship instantly and hope to take the alien ship with it. None of the other members on that team were particularly keen to volunteer for another space flight with that captain!

However, even the practical steps of the above example are not lost – look again at the fishbone and, apart from one or two specific questions, you will see that they are questions that would be relevant to, say, the US president and the Russian president in discussing trust-building for nuclear arms limitation. Look at the fishbone again and consider its relevance to companies forced to work with their own competitors. For example, petrol companies may be forced to sell competitor's brands on their own forecourts; how would such companies build trust between themselves?

No one is suggesting that the ability to fly a spaceship is a requirement for industry; what are important are the processes of radical thinking that exercises like these develop in team members. From experience we have seen that using 'fun' programmes makes the learning more memorable and effective.

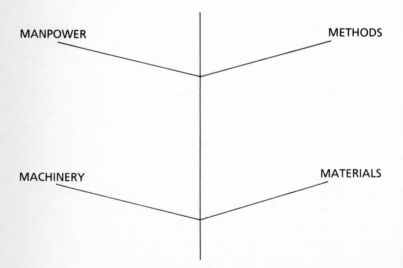

For general business problem solving in teams the application of the fishbone is often called the '4 Ms' method, or cause-and-effect diagrams. The 4 Ms are manpower, materials, methods and machinery. The problem is defined within these four categories so as to reach agreement about where the team feels the problem arises and consequently where to concentrate the energy and resources. This has the advantage of accelerating the brainstorming process without losing the synergy.

6.   PROJECT OWNERSHIP

'By the splendour of God I have taken possession of my
realm; the earth of England is in my two hands'.

William the Conqueror

A current buzz-phrase commonly heard in our organisation is
'bought in'. The team leaders are frequently asking the team
members, 'Have you bought in on this?' This concept of ownership is not new, but to hear management in discussions you
would have thought that it had just been discovered. Did the
slaves of ancient Egypt 'buy into' the building of the pyramids or
the temples of the Gods? To some extent we can argue that they
probably did 'buy into' the temples, as keeping the Gods happy
was necessary for their well-being. No doubt medieval labourers
bought into the building of their lord's castle as they knew that
when trouble arose their lord would defend them, since they were
often within the safety in the castle walls. But ownership must be
more than a function of security or worship. Business managers
are requiring more ownership of tasks and projects from the
workforce, the workforce is organised into teams, therefore our
teams have to own the project or process.

In return for this we offer degrees of remuneration and security
in its many forms. How then can we instil a sense of ownership
into the team? Let us examine in general what we mean by
ownership. What do we know about things we own? Ownership
will normally arise from say a purchase, a gift, or something we
have made or discovered.

If we buy something we know we have title to, we own it. We
can do with it what we please, up to a point. Society quite rightly
makes rules about what we can do with the things we own; we can

own a gun, but we can't go around shooting at people. Similarly with a gift; within the rules we can do what we like with it, but a gift has more connotations than something we purchase, a gift may have sentimental or emotional value that stops us from using it or disposing of it, even when it is broken, or we are offered money for it.

Something we have made or discovered is altogether different; if we discover something we may have an attachment to it that goes well beyond the concept of ownership by mere purchase or gift.

So, can the above singular ideas have any use in teambuilding? The answer must be a categorical 'Yes'. In most project work, the tasks and objectives to be undertaken are handed to the team. In a similar manner the team may purchase a project, perhaps by bidding for it, and offering themselves as the best people to do the job. They will be nominally rewarded for doing the job, but to release the extra energy so often needed to do an excellent job, as opposed to just getting away with it, they will then go beyond their contractual obligations if they feel they have, through effort, purchased the right to do the job. By winning the right to do the job, the project has to be more meaningful for them. They may well have had to fight off competition to get the project and this will give them a sense of achievement; put simply, what we win we own and it means more to us.

Let us now look at the example of a gift. If we give a project to a team does this have a higher or lower impact than the purchase method of ownership? Giving out work, i.e. projects, to a team without consultation, as opposed to the team having to earn the right, may well lessen the ability of the team to take full ownership. In our daily lives we may be given gifts, but apart from the sentiment or emotion felt, often the gifts are useless to us. What matters here, then, is not the gift, but the way it was given.

While working for an American consultancy group, one of the authors was seconded to various different teams, often as team leader. On one occasion we were called in by the MD and given the 'gift' of a project which we then had to sell to the project team. We had not been given the opportunity to win the project, and initial findings indicated that the project was both interesting and challenging. At the same time another team leader was given another project, apparently just as interesting and challenging.

The main difference between the two projects was that one was in Norway and the other was in the North-west of England. Professionalism would have demanded that either project would have been executed in the highest standard required, but the length of time that the project teams took to commit to ownership of the project was different.

The Norway-bound team took immediate ownership, the gift of the project here was a plum. My team, North-west England bound, took a little longer to take ownership as they too would have liked the chance of foreign travel. If we could have competed with the other team for the Norway project and lost, it would have made the ownership of the other project easier to grasp.

Discovery or development of the project, in our experience, instils an even deeper sense of ownership from day one, 'It is our brainchild, it is our idea'. When we hear these words we know ownership is in place. For this reason making our teams part of the initial planning process of the potential project gives those teams the ability to take part in the discovery process.

So, what can we learn about the above three forms of project ownership?

First, in the example of winning the right to the project we have introduced the elements of effort and challenge. This instils a sense of ownership and unites the team. The drawback here is that in order to quote for the project the clearly defined lines of the project had to be drawn up. So although the team is possibly motivated to ownership, they may not be happy with what they are now seeing has to be done. This can cause problems with the project in that they will begin to 'own' the parts of the project they like and 'reject' the bits they don't like, their excuse being 'Well, these bits were foisted upon us'.

Secondly, where the project is a gift from management, management itself will have to set clearly the boundary rules of the project. A gift with restrictions that have not been negotiated is a gift that may be unused.

The advantage of the third method, of discovering or developing, is that the project is not clearly defined at the outset. It is being built up. And the objectives can only be stated and discussed at a minimum level. The project then becomes a voyage of discovery on how to do the job; the team will buy into the project because they are making the rules as they go along (obviously within the boundary limits). The tasks and objectives are not then just a collection of delegated functions, but also a team plan where every team member can have, or has had, input of their particular skills, and the team members have decided among themselves who shall do what and with what.

This we can now describe as a more empowered form of ownership, and this needs a braver form of management than the control form of handing down work. Management's job at this point in the process will be to give to the team all the necessary permissions and authorities so that the team can do the job with a minimum of interference.

We have worked on such projects where the task was communicated with the end result needed. In one particular case, as team leaders we were told that we had to take a percentage of savings out of the overheads of an organisation by a certain date, so that the organisation's bankers would be able to continue to support the client. The team was called together and given the problem, i.e. we know what we want, how do we do it? Immediate ownership was forged with individual members of the team stating their strengths arising out of past experiences and in particular their skills in reducing the costs of certain departments. A plan was quickly formed and individual team members went away for a day to come back to the team with a tactical plan for each department. The cost savings were achieved quicker than originally planned and we more than doubled the savings requested by the client.

How, then, can this be interpreted by the manager for use in their organisation? Our submission is that the speed and depth of ownership, from our experience, is often in direct correlation with the amount of information given to the team to do the task. If the team is allowed to make up its own rules about how to do the job quicker ownership will ensue. If teams are treated robotically, the skills and professionalism will still be there, but ownership will not be as quick or as strong. The challenge to management is that when a team is formed to do a job the first consideration to be addressed is: does ownership apply here? For some projects ownership may not be necessary, but if ownership is essential then the team must decide how to do the work.

Let us now turn to the situation where ownership is not established and the team only functions at a task or skills level. If

97

a team has not bought into the project then not only is commitment lacking, but the lack of ownership will also be communicated by the team to all people having dealings with it, and this will affect the quality of the transactions as non-ownership will spread outwards in all directions. The authors have spent a considerable amount of time working with teams on total quality management (TQM) projects. One of the main drivers of TQM in any organisation is total commitment from top management to the process. In one particular client, work groups for problem solving have been established and the differences between the work groups who have bought into and established ownership of the process and those who have not, are decidedly marked. Let us look at the characteristics of the groups with and without ownership.

Teams who have taken ownership

- Meet as directed, in this case every two weeks for two hours, but often meet *ad hoc* in order to progress the tasks.

- Did not need a formal agenda, but set a brief agenda at the outset of the meeting enabling enthusiastic team members to capture the meeting with the most interesting challenge offered on that day.

- Insisted on making successes public through the house magazine, and also insisted on making visible partial success (better than partial failure), so that other people in the organisation could offer possible solutions and ideas to the team.

- Kept only brief minutes, but did file with them detailed plans and results so that the methodology could be reused for similar types of problem solving.

- Only dealt with problems relating to the team's tasks and avoided discussions to do with hygiene factors, company policy and personnel matters.

- Co-opted into meetings experts and representatives of sup-

pliers and customers when dealing with problems that inter-
faced with them.

- Constantly sought new training for its team, particularly in
communications and problem-solving methods.

Teams who have not taken ownership

- Meet only as directed with absenteeism ranging from 20 to 30
per cent in most instances. Very rarely discussed issues outside
the formal meeting venue.

- Constructed detailed and formal agendas with times against
each subject to be discussed. Any new items were added by
rote so that a new idea may take three to four months to get to
the stage when the group would deal with it.

- Insisted on making public successes through the house
magazine and often asking management for tangible forms of
recognition. Unwillingness to publicise failed or partially failed
projects.

- Kept detailed minutes with action comments alongside. Working papers and flow diagrams of the problem-solving process
and methodology normally not retained.

- Dealt with all problems ranging from tasks of the group, personnel problems, health and safety, and hygiene factors to the
politics of the organisation.

- Held meetings in closed session with no co-option from within
or without the organisation.

- Ambivalent attitude towards training and only saw necessity
for skills training, usually for a new piece of technology.

The reader will see that at the functional level both teams will
solve problems, but the team with ownership, by concentrating
and putting all of its energies into beating the problem, is the one
that will add value to its organisation in the quickest period of
time.

7. STRENGTHS, WEAKNESSES, VALUES AND PREJUDICES

'Somehow every organisation must make room for inner-directed, obstreperous, creative people, sworn enemies of routine and the status quo, always ready to upset the apple cart by thinking up new and better ways of doing things.'

Admiral Hyman G. Rickover

Strengths and weaknesses of team members

From the moment we first go to school we are used to being organised into teams. Many of us may not have regarded forms or school houses as a primitive attempt to instil teambuilding into our formative years; but over a period of time, especially through sport, we began to recognise teams and the strengths and weaknesses of individual team members. In business we are formed into teams by whatever name (division, department, sections) and we are all given team leaders. Teams of long standing know the strengths and weaknesses of team members, as these have been teased out over a period of time and the team can bask in the sunlight of mutual understanding.

The acceptance by organisations of quick response teams to tackle specific problems has uncovered a fundamental weakness of newly formed teams in that often the team members do not know the strengths and weaknesses of the individual team members or how they are to learn these in those first formative meetings.

For this reason it will be necessary, if not essential, to allow the newly formed teams to conduct teambuilding exercises, and also for long-standing teams to re-learn the strengths and weaknesses of team members. Teambuilding exercises to establish acceptance of these issues should be regarded as an investment. In this chapter we shall look at some of the traditional methods used and describe some new methods that we have developed in our client companies.

The methods we shall look at are described as follows:

- the morning disclosure sessions ('Prayer meetings');
- the hotel bar method;
- brainstorming exercises;
- problem-solving exercises;
- other management games;
- outward-bound courses.

The morning disclosure sessions

In the early 1980s one of the authors of this book was working in the USA for an American consulting company as a member of various teams. Most of the teams did not know each other well, and were recruited from across the USA, from differing backgrounds with different skills. Much of the work was conducted by individuals on their own or working with the client's staff. Every morning we as a team would meet with our team leader and each one of us would have to declare to the team how our individual tasks were going, what strengths we were bringing to the solutions of the problems, and what weaknesses we had and how this was affecting our work. We were also encouraged to discuss our relationship with fellow team members and how we could help them. At first this was a disturbing experience, especially for a Brit who was not used to the level of personal disclosure asked for by American colleagues, and certainly not used to making such issues public.

However, during the months spent with different project teams, it became clear that this was a very effective form of teambuilding. Every time a strength or weakness was exposed it gave a fellow team member or members the opportunity to support, encourage and make constructive comments about an individual's skill, work or social attitude. On one very notable occasion a very sensitive and caring member of the team confessed to feeling very uneasy in the particular implementation of a strategy that would lead to the sacking of people he had been working with. Immediately, a team member offered to assist by setting up an outplacement service with the client for their staff. That member of the team had, before joining that project, been a line-manager in an outplacement organisation and up to this point had not made it common knowledge, as he wanted to be recognised by the team for a different set of skills. When it came to the crunch, however, he increased his personal disclosure to help a fellow team member in trouble.

The hotel bar method

A few summers ago one of the authors was running work-group leader training sessions for a large UK multinational as part of their total quality initiative. In most companies we have worked in, such training is regarded as functional and, under the guise of cost restraint, delegates are nominated to a training room during normal working hours.

In this particular case the manager responsible decided to make the training course residential, and thus – and in fact by accident – instil some elements of teambuilding into the training sessions. He decided that the benefits would outweigh the extra cost involved. Thus, the delegates would meet the night before, for dinner, a few drinks and discussion afterwards. This obviously gave the team members a chance to meet socially, and discuss a wide range of work and non-work issues. The impact upon the course was very noticeable; the level of discussion, challenge to the issues and teambuilding exercises were above the level observed in those using the classroom medium. To our mind this is an excellent example of teambuilding in an informal manner with very little added investment.

Brainstorming exercises

Depending upon the skill of the team leader and the degree of openness and honesty within the organisation, the use of brain-storming sessions (often called 'away days' in business) are a very effective form of teambuilding. Sometimes, and recommended by us, team leaders will wish to take part in the sessions themselves and then it is sensible to use an outside agent to lead the sessions and synthesise the results. Such sessions are best held on neutral ground so that any association with line responsibilities and rank are kept to a minimum. After a few short warm-up exercises the group should set its own agenda and encourage as radical a thinking process as possible. A sense of fun and the ridiculous should be encouraged at all levels of the process, as that enables team members to use parts of their brain which are normally kept closed.

From our experience most brainstorming sessions fail if the group is not willing to test the boundary limits of the organisation, and the leader is unable to infuse into the process the degree of recklessness needed. True brainstorming sessions should cross departmental boundaries with all rank removed and, while it should not turn into the 'office party', it should be a free and honest exchange of views on the chosen subjects. The leader should have the necessary confidence in the team and himself to tease out the underlying gripes of the organisation, as well as then moving the level of interaction to constructive criticism, and 'What can we do now?' attitudes. The ice-breaking, warm-up sessions should be as humorous and challenging as possible; we have used such exercises as 'Two minutes to come up with fifty things to do with a hard-boiled egg'. To avoid restricting answers to such obvious comments as 'Eat it', the facilitator can offer the first, say, 'Make a punk earring'. The tone is set!

Problem-solving exercises

People, and people in teams, like solving problems with the sense of achievement that goes with it. Problem solving in groups affect teambuilding as individual team members can recognise who enters into the debate, and when they do so, which can then be noted for future reference. Solving problems are a tangible exercise which people can get their teeth into, as well as giving individual members the chance to air their knowledge and expertise. The responsibility of the team leader in these sessions is to facilitate the process by introducing and reminding the team of problem-solving techniques, i.e. fishbone analysis (which we have seen in Chapter 5), computer modelling and the many other techniques which are used; but in particular those techniques commonly in place in the organisation.

Other management games

As we have seen, all exercises with people are teambuilding, and the amount of theoretical and practical games in the market place is legion. Management games can be split into three categories, bought in theoretical, bought in practical, and do-it-yourself.

Bought in theoretical

These are normally of a general nature where the leader, after a brief introduction, splits the group into smaller teams if necessary, and then debriefs the team afterwards. The advantage of these games is that because they are tried and tested, and usually well thought out, the leader does not have to do very much up-front work, and the debrief is vague and flexible enough to satisfy everyone's needs. The other great advantage is that games are neutral, which avoids the team getting locked into the organisational issues.

From our experience, these games are often regarded as unreal by the players and it takes a lot of skill and experience from the facilitator to get the best out of them. We have seen some excellent games played very well by teams, only to be deflated by inexperienced facilitators who cannot identify the lessons to be learned. The prime purpose of theoretical games is the teambuilding process and the identification of roles emerging; not the speed, accuracy or sensibility of the result.

Bought in practical

Here again there are many in the market place that can be bought off the shelf. The facilitator's skill here is to understand exactly what conclusions he or she wishes to demonstrate through the process. Too many games, to our mind, are just a form of jigsaw puzzle with some communication exercises built in. They will no doubt engender some form of teambuilding at the practical level, especially if a competitive element is introduced (i.e. against the clock or another team), but often are best left to the Jackanory school of management (games for games' sake). Practical games are an important part of teambuilding, but rarely do they stand alone, and should only be used to reinforce a theoretical concept.

Do-it-yourself

Team leaders, often with help from the training department, should be able to devise their own theoretical and practical games, and in some cases other people's games can be used as a guideline. The great advantage of making up your own games is ownership and all the benefits that ownership brings. The do-it-yourself games can have a necessary blend of realism without overtly getting into the swamp of organisational issues that will hinder the process. Also, self-made games can be devised with the individual team members' strengths and weaknesses built in. On the practical side, the particular skills of the team, say, engineering or distribution, can be the backcloth against which the game is built. For the leader it does take up-front work, but as in so many tasks the up-front investment in time is rewarded in the process by the team, the realism in the task and the ease of interpreting the results.

Outward-bound courses

Many companies and organisations are investing in the increasingly popular management outward-bound courses. In this context we have debriefed many managers at all levels of the organisation. The courses on offer range from war games with paint- or radar-guns, to more structured courses with specific team tasks, i.e. raft building and sporting activities. Conflict of opinion arises as to the best form of course, but most people we have met who have been on such courses have enjoyed themselves. Some courses take individuals from various organisations and forge them into a team, for perhaps a week. The benefit to the individual is that he or she learns more about his or her strengths and weaknesses in a team situation than would otherwise be possible, and this should make that person a better team player for the future. The danger is that the individual does not like what has been learnt and may well hide their weaknesses and only push the strengths.

Other forms of courses take new or old existing teams and by working them together, and against themselves and nature, they learn more about each other and their team. From our discussions into such activities it would seem that many people going on them volunteer or, with colleagues, engineer getting a course organised or funded. (If they can take such a decision as a team they have probably demonstrated that they don't need the course!) Many people admitted having little or no enthusiasm for the idea, but because the exercises were fun they enjoyed it. In some cases, they also discovered skills, e.g. woodwork or cooking, that they did not know they had.

Has the development of such skills, personal enjoyment of tasks and primitive living conditions got anything to do with teambuilding in a modern organisation? Building a raft in a given time and crossing a river on it may do wonders for one's self-esteem and sense of team achievement, but what has this to do with the compilation of a budget or making decisions regarding cost-cutting or market strategy?

One of the problems here, then, is that these 'armed services' ideas of teambuilding are no doubt excellent for training the troops, keeping them fit and helping to develop their own sense of strengths and weaknesses, but where are the risk issues, where the only risk is getting shot with washable paint, or getting wet and then being saved by the course organiser?

Most managers, to our mind, can benefit from outward-bound courses as they can discover strengths and weaknesses about themselves and their team, depending on the course. But most of these lessons can be learned by the problems that arise in just trying to catch a plane from Heathrow airport at the height of the summer season!

In order to develop and understand teambuilding games and other vehicles to discover acceptance and visibility of strengths and weaknesses, we must be very clear that when we do discover them we have the expertise and back-up to do something with them. In many situations the exposure of weakness is a hindrance to the team; such weaknesses must be addressed and talked out, and corrected through counselling and training. Strengths must be built upon through training and practice. The whole concept of teambuilding is to unite the team and to stop it breaking ranks under threat. We must, therefore, at some stage in the team's growth, establish a menu with the members, of the acceptable strengths and weaknesses we can live with, what corrective action to take and at what expense we will live with each other in the workplace.

Values and prejudices of team members

In order for a team to knit together there must be acceptance and knowledge of the values and prejudices of the team members. In the past this was not as much of a problem as it is today. Certainly, before the Second World War, labour mobility was geographically confined, so that most people would end up working near where they were born. The exceptions were, of course, London and some major industrial conurbations which have always attracted people from different areas. This presented no problem for the team leader, as most of the people in the team came from the same area, went to the same schools, read the same books and understood the local culture. This meant that they all readily acknowledged each other's values and prejudices as they were all similar, and anyone who did not agree with the team's values, attitudes and beliefs was obviously not quite right in the head and could be tolerated because they were the odd one out.

The current situation in most areas has now changed. There have been major social upheavals, immigration, a re-think of social values; managers and team leaders are being drawn from different social areas and backgrounds. There are still some 'islands' within our islands in the UK. Hull, for example, has often been described as an island off the coast of England. Where you have a community like Hull, and similarly in parts of Wales and Scotland, there is a common thread of values and prejudices that are easily recognisable. Even here the castle walls are being pulled down and teambuilding exercises are being developed in order that the team can recognise and accept, where possible, the differences.

The North–South divide, made so much of in the press, is cultural as well as economic, and it is difficult for many managers to accept the values and prejudices of the South being exported to the North (and vice versa) through the vehicle of a corporate centre. Many times we have had discussions with managers and team leaders who complain that those in 'London' have no idea of the people they are trying to manage. The Japanese have taught us that in many of their factories in the West, they do not try and change the culture of the workforce, but they often insist on putting into the workplace the disciplines, working methods and supervision necessary to do the job. Many of the UK companies that we are working in are still trying to change the culture of the organisation without first having learned and understood the existing culture and the values of such a culture. Often, by changing the culture, we may be removing one of the fundamental pillars that held the organisation up in the first place.

What type of values and prejudices do we now have to consider in our organisations and institutions, and have they changed radically over the past decade? One of the more noticeable effects of Thatcherism was the perception of the Yuppie society in the South by the North. This meant that any young person who dressed in a particular way or drove a certain type of car was accredited with a set of values and prejudices that had been invented by the media.

These young people then found themselves having to defend their values in teams and this has caused at least short-term disruption in building teams. Some of our larger and more traditional industries have only recently discovered that 50 per cent of the population is female and it is still rare to see female apprentices in the so-called hard trades. Many of these same companies will not invest in crêches for young mothers; instead they prefer to see them leave the organisation, albeit for a period of time, rather than consolidate their investment by keeping them at the workplace. Such values and prejudices are not helped by our political masters who act as if they believe, and occasionally they state outright, that women should stay at home and bring up their children. The return to the so-called Victorian values has done a great deal to undermine the progress being made in acceptance of new values in our organisations.

Earlier, we considered the strengths and weaknesses of team members that have to be discovered if the team is to function to its maximum potential. In a similar way we must now discuss the route to be taken to discover the values and prejudices of the individual team members so that the team can work together without upsetting the line of acceptance and rejection. Some values and prejudices are all too obvious in any organisation and, as they are easily recognisable, they can usually be managed very simply. If a person is a committed 'Green', then it might be very difficult for that person to work in a team that produces toxic waste that is then dumped in the river. If that person chooses to do so, taking the line advocated by, say, Tony Benn of 'fight-for-change-from-within' the organisation, then so long as the team tolerates those views he or she can contribute to the team in an effective manner.

Obviously, in many instances, these matters rarely become critical because we have human resource specialists who devise strategies and psychometric tests so that people with a profile that may upset a team are filtered out at the interview and selection stage. However, people are getting good at these tests and we have come across many people whose code of life is no doubt at loggerheads with the organisations they have joined. Another problem is that the organisation changes its values and prejudices at the top in full recognition that the workforce have not changed theirs. Environmental and Common Market issues are examples where management are often, through no fault of their own, imposing a new set of rules upon the teams.

Let us now look at how the spectrum of values and prejudices that we can recognise in organisations can be unearthed by the team.

What, then, can we as team leaders do to raise the visibility of such issues, bring them into open debate so that we can begin the process of rejection of what is not acceptable and the acceptance of what is needed? One of the popular teambuilding exercises that teases out the values and prejudices is based on saving people from difficult and potentially fatal (imagined) situations. In these types of games the team has to decide who to save first. The people profiles demonstrate positive and negative attributes of the individuals, and having run the exercise many teams can then learn what is acceptable and unacceptable to their group.

We can now turn our attention to psychometric testing as a vehicle for establishing values and prejudices. For those of us who have been through such exercises, we know it is purely to establish if we are a fit and proper person to join the organisation, and in particular the team we are trying to enter. But do teams have their own psychometric profiles, do they use them and should they use them? In fact should the team be able to influence who is to join them? The jury is still out on this one. We do a lot of work with young graduates in the training room on a number of management skills programmes, and often it does not matter which organisation we are working in, the recruitment patterns are all too similar. On a recent induction course, even before walking into the room we knew we would encounter a mix of ex-head girls and boys, the odd Operation Raleigh graduate and captains of various sports. As we discussed in Chapter 3, God-like qualities are what we would like our leaders to have, but do we know enough about the values and prejudices by which they will operate in teams?

Can we discover how many are satanists, fascists, or communists, how many woman-haters, or man-haters, and all the other facets of the human individual which may or may not be acceptable to the team members. Is it necessary? Or can we argue that real problem values and real problem prejudices are so narrowly distributed across the population that we can afford the odd one or two? Also, do these tests actually bring out these issues or are our new recruits getting good at pulling the wool over our eyes, by concealing from us what they really think. The organisation can construct a psychological map of its workforce and can then best fit people to it, but from our experience the team will, in time, uncover the real person behind the mask and will either accept, or reject or try to change that person. The team has, if it is working properly, the ability and strength to cope with people who think differently from other individuals and in many cases can use such differences to advantage.

As front-line trainers we work with groups for short periods of time, say two to four days. These people are often not used to working together, so the trainer's first work is to unite the team. This can be done most easily by challenging the group through their core values and prejudices, and challenging a few 'sacred cows' in the organisation. By consistent challenge the team will readily unite against the trainer and rise to the defence of the group, and from then on the trainer can work with the group relaxing the challenges and thereby the tension, but the group will remain knitted together, and will normally remain so. A word of caution though, you have to be well practised at this form of group work as there is a fine line between uniting the group and alienating yourself from it.

The training forum is therefore a very effective way of bringing out values and prejudices by challenging the traditional stances that you know people hold most dear. Another and possibly easier route for the team leader is to run a personal disclosure group meeting to tease out the common ground, showing that individual members of the team have a great deal more in common than they previously thought. When they realise that they are all the same, they will begin to relax and think of themselves as more of a team. In some organisations where we work we start such an exercise like fortune tellers by informing the group what they have in common. With practice this is easy to do and we know from our experience that in a group of say ten to twelve people in the age group twenty-four to thirty the majority will have the following common ground:

Favourite colour	Blue
Favourite food	Curry
Favourite pastime	Cinema/pub
Favourite reading	Little or not at all!
Favourite holiday	Fell walking
Favourite hobby	Decorating
and so on. . .	

How, then, can we address the issues and make them work to our advantage? Put simply, in the formative stages of the team development, some time must be given for the members of the team to express their values and prejudices. People want to talk about themselves and they want to find common ground with the rest of their team. Often they want to shock; they will do this to test the parameters, so that they can readily establish what is and what is not acceptable to the fellow team members. Remember that our schools and colleges are producing, and always have produced, people who have a great deal in common with each other. We know this and all we have to do is enable them to demonstrate and learn themselves that they are no different, and any great differences can be left to form alliances with like-minded people in a social sense.

The last issue then is how do we, having now discovered the values and prejudices of our team members, correct such prejudices as are unacceptable to the team and reinforce such values that are considered to be key drivers to the success of the team? This has to be done through behavioural training. Behaviour is the only part of us that is visible to our fellow team members. We demonstrate our values and prejudices by what we do, what we say and by what we wear. If we wear badges in support of any kind of group, e.g. political, religious or action group, we are demonstrating our beliefs openly to the world. If we act in such a way that upsets the team, then the team must have the right to correct such action by pointing out the effect of such actions upon others. If a member of the team is consistently late for meetings, then that person must be told that their behaviour is totally unacceptable to the team, and they must change that behaviour, otherwise the team may well remove them. Similarly, the way a person communicates verbally; if it has an adverse effect on the team then it may be necessary for that person to undergo influence skills training.

In conclusion, we must remember that values and prejudices are not genetic, they are taught to us by our family, friends, schools and literature. We are having to function in very mixed teams these days, and while we must – as the old adage goes – respect the views of others, we cannot work to maximum effect with people whose views are so far removed from ours that they become a hindrance to the teams, as energy is then spent settling such differences rather than the task on hand. For this reason it is better to counsel the individual if he has views and values that are so beyond society's norms that he keeps them hidden, as long as by doing so he is not being dishonest and is not incorrectly influencing the team in the wrong direction.

In working with groups and examining this question of values and prejudices we have used several 'games' to draw out the points considered above. One such 'game' is the Scholarship Committee.

The Scholarship Committee

The purpose of this game is to enable members of a team to discover and accept the values and prejudices of fellow team members. For this reason the character traits have been deliberately exaggerated to the point of creating 'cardboard' stereotypes. Values and prejudices are serious matters and there must be the release of emotion through humour, or these games can get too serious, and create conflict. The game is not designed to change values in the short term, but rather to allow people to identify them in themselves, which is the start of behavioural change.

Methodology

Any number of people can participate, preferably split into groups within the range of four to eight delegates.

The course/team leader should distribute a copy of the briefing sheet and a synopsis of the applications for the Scholarships.

Each group should elect a team leader for the purpose of this task who, at the end of the game, should feed back results and issues raised to all course participants (including other groups).

As a guideline, ten minutes should be sufficient to read the briefing sheet and applicants details, and thirty to forty-five minutes should be allowed to complete the task.

Scholarship Committee briefing sheet

You are an academic group of teachers at a polytechnic in the heart of England. Your college awards four scholarships per annum, based on the selection you arrive at from the candidates offered. The scholarships to be awarded are as follows:

Alpha: £6,000 per annum
Beta: £4,000 per annum
Gamma: £2,000 per annum
Delta: £1,000 per annum

The heads of departments have submitted to you a shortlist of ten candidates.

Your task as a committee is to award the scholarships for the next academic year.

Details of the applicants are as follows

DUNCAN
Duncan is eighteen years old, unmarried and wishes to study for a degree in chemical engineering. He was born in a very deprived area of Glasgow and was brought up by his mother as his father ran away with another woman when he was twelve. Duncan's hobbies are mountain climbing and socialising in pubs. He is a

member of the Celtic Socialist Workers Organisation and has been arrested on two separate occasions for disturbances of the peace at public demonstrations.

SHAKA

Shaka is a mature student aged forty-two, married with six children. His wife and children live in Suweto. He has applied to study anthropology and social sciences. Shaka was born in Suweto and presently lives in Notting Hill Gate, where he has a job working for a fast-food hamburger chain. Shaka is currently having an overt sexual relationship in this country and at his interview has indicated that he does not wish to return home. His interests are prison visiting and he runs a youth club for the disabled.

LIA WAN

Lia Wan is twenty-four years old and already holds a degree in English from the University of Hong Kong. Lia Wan is an unmarried mother whose daughter is looked after by her grandmother. She has applied to study for an MA in romantic poetry. Lia Wan's hobbies are volleyball and cooking. Lia Wan is astoundingly attractive and has indicated at interview that she has discovered she prefers the company of women. She is an active member of a feminist pressure group.

ALVIN

Alvin is thirty years of age, divorced. He has two children, who live with their mother. Alvin's father is the junior senator for a western State of the USA, who is also a multi-millionaire. Alvin already has a degree in sociology and has applied to study for a degree in modern European languages. Alvin has indicated that although his father is prepared to pay for his college course, he is unwilling to ask him to do so and is therefore seeking the scholarship. He has recently been diagnosed as HIV positive.

FLACCA

Flacca is nineteen years old and is the unmarried daughter of a South American general supporting a particularly oppressive regime. She is a committed Roman Catholic and apart from her convent education has never lived outside her family ranch. Her hobbies are sewing and horse-riding. Flacca wishes to study military history and politics. Her ambition is to enter politics in her own country and she admits to being right wing in her political thinking.

ROSE
Rose is a mature student who has just completed her studies during her three-year prison sentence for embezzlement. Rose is aged forty-seven, married with no children. During the interview Rose stated that she went to prison to protect her husband. Her hobbies are teaching English to foreign students and she is an auxiliary nurse in a local hospice. Rose has applied for a postgraduate diploma in English.

CLAUDE
Claude is a twenty-six-year-old Frenchman currently living in London with Jean-Luc, a fifty-six-year-old retired schoolmaster. Their relationship is stable. Claude has spent the last four years achieving the necessary qualifications to apply for college and wishes to study theology with a view to entering the priesthood. His hobbies are keeping house and cooking. Claude supports his ageing mother in France by working in a factory on night-shifts.

MAUREEN
Maureen is a forty-five-year-old schoolteacher who wishes to study for a degree in mathematics. Maureen has two grown-up daughters and has refused to answer any other personal questions. The interviewers' notes state that she is quiet and reserved, and somewhat intolerant of people. She is highly intelligent and articulate. She presently teaches mathematics to nine and ten year olds, and wishes to continue doing so.

BAZ
Baz is a twenty-two-year-old Australian who wishes to study for a degree in psychology. He is unmarried and lives alone in Earl's Court, London. Baz has written a book on the history of Australian lager and is high priest of a coven of witches dedicated to the Moon-Goddess. Baz has recently been expelled from an ecology-based pressure group because he stood for local council elections on the platform of decimating rainforests to provide

growing areas for cannabis, which he believes should be legalised. Baz is a member of MENSA, with an IQ of 148.

ZARA
Zara is a twenty-six-year-old investment banker who has applied to read for an MBA specialising in financial services. Zara is ex-chair of the Young Conservatives, London Students Branch. Her hobbies are politics, cricket and motor racing. She is currently living with the director of a merchant bank and is four months pregnant. Zara speaks three languages and is part-owner of a wine bar in Chelsea. She is a counsellor for an alcoholics recovery centre.

The course tutors' role is to highlight the values and prejudices that arise from the selection process. From experience certain team members will favour the 'traditional' values and condemn those who have taken drugs, become unmarried parents and so on, but equally there will be those who believe they are taking an enlightened line by deliberately selecting just those candidates. Both ends of the spectrum must be shown that they are exhibiting prejudicial thinking and responding to stereotypes (which the examples blatantly are!) and are making decisions based on their own experiences or beliefs.

8. TECHNIQUES DEVELOPED FROM THE NON-BUSINESS WORLD

'We never do anything well till we cease to think about the manner of doing it.'

William Hazlitt

One theory of management is that less time spent 'playing' leaves more time for 'doing' and in fact business allows for very little play, or what we call rehearsal, time. By increasing the time spent developing the team, the team becomes more effective in its real-time work. It may have less time for action, but it will produce more in the time available.

There is a disparity between rehearsal time for business where there might be a half-hour briefing for a meeting on which a valuable contract depends and such time in, say, the performing arts, where it is not unusual to have three weeks' rehearsal for one night's performance. None the less, rehearsal is the basis of putting together any quick response team that needs to get an effective job done quickly.

Team leaders with management trainers have long recognised that an important part of the relationship between team members relies on building trust. To some extent this has always been allowed to develop in its own right, because it has been believed that there was time for this to happen. Where a team has a long-term life of many years, then trust was allowed to build up in a haphazard way as the team progressed through the **READY–STEADY–GO** stages.

However, the modern business world is a situation of corporate decisions in a constant climate of change and the majority of proactive teams are quick response or corrective action teams formed to deal with an immediate problem. As such the **READY**

117

and **STEADY** stages must be accelerated so that the team 'hits the ground running'. This has created a problem for team trainers who are having to come to grips with the requirements of instant proactive teams.

We have been at the forefront of a revolutionary form of management training involving a close interplay between the business world and members of the performing arts. This has proved a remarkably successful partnership. Only a moment's thought will explain why; actors as a group, and particularly theatre performers, are very used to the problems of being a disunited group of individuals – indeed individuality is one of the vitally important aspects of their character. However, they must be able to group together very quickly in a performance company, unite with a common purpose, perform that purpose with excellence, and still be able to break up, go elsewhere and form other teams. In short, they already exhibit all the attributes required by quick response and corrective action teams.

The problem for trainers was how to reconcile the business world and the artistic world. In fact, the reconciliation was far easier than expected as the established paradigms had already begun to break down some time before. In the business world it was long recognised that the most enterprising business people were not staid conservative automatons seeking profit for profit's sake at all expense, and with their feet firmly planted in the eighteenth century. Many of today's business people show the same kind of creativity and flair which, in fact, the acting profession often desperately seek; Sir John Harvey Jones is an obvious example that comes to mind. On the other hand the acting profession was no longer seen as, indeed no longer consisted of, airy-fairy people with their heads in the clouds. As self-employed people they were running their own businesses and some were doing so with remarkable business-like efficiency. They were applying to their own circumstances the business principles of cost-effectiveness and profit, together with their own natural creative energies.

The combination of the two in training has been irresistible; perhaps the most obvious comes with presentation skills or performance skills where courses we have run have included both the technical skills of presentation, together with the acting skills of performance. In business skills training, influencing skills and report writing, for example, the business world has provided the guidelines, while the acting profession has offered much of the flair and creativity that produces effective impact.

In teambuilding the energies have come together as never before. Many of the teambuilding skills which arise from the business world have been discussed in other chapters. The skills required to generate trust come mainly from the performing arts and some of these techniques are described below.

Establish the ground rules

In any training session where such personal aspects as trust between individuals are to be dealt with there must be clear ground rules. First, there will have to be intimate disclosure by individuals and it must be made clear from the outset that any information gleaned will be strictly confidential. This is important enough where individuals are not known to each other, perhaps attending open training courses, but it is even more vital inside a company where the participants are known to each other. At the end of the day all the participants will have put something of themselves into the course and therefore are all equally vulnerable; as a consequence this trust is almost always respected. For those who break the trust it is much the same as any 'politicking' during meetings or team work; the person doing so becomes known for their attitude and inevitably it backfires on them.

Secondly, there must be no criticism – either overtly or covertly. People will be asked to disclose very personal information which may possibly be something that breaks certain social conventions. The ground rules must state that no one will attack or question such disclosure directly or, as importantly, by gesture or expression. Again, this is usually accepted by participants, provided the team trainer is skilled at putting people at ease. It is a point worth saying that it is usually an external trainer called in for this purpose because of the neutrality of his or her position, but it can also be achieved by the team leader. Inevitably, if this is to be the case, then the best approach the team leader can make is to be the first actually to make a disclosure of the nature he or she wants from the other participants; such leadership almost always instantly succeeds.

Eye contact

Many people in a group, and particularly when they are first brought together, set up a barrier by avoiding eye contact with each other. The group should be encouraged to stand in a circle and each person should make direct eye contact with every other person in the circle, one at a time, at their own random choice. Eye contact should last for perhaps one minute, after which the person should say 'Thank you' and then move on to the next person. The contacts must be mutual and this can easily be achieved as all members of the circle are seeking eye contact with the others. It will take some minutes before everyone has achieved eye contact with everyone else, but this is the beginning of a warming to each other which is essential for this kind of session.

The most traumatic or upsetting moment

Each individual in turn, with possibly the team leader first, is asked to describe to the group, in detail, the most traumatic and upsetting event of their lives. It may seem, in cold black and white, that it will be difficult to get people to disclose such personal information. In fact, this is not the case and, indeed, in our experience of doing these workshops, it seems that many people are almost seeking an audience where the above two rules have been made paramount. Fairly run-of-the-mill disclosures include accidents that have resulted in significant fear which the person then feels ashamed of (in one case a woman described being on a canoeing expedition and hitting severe white water and having to be rescued after coming within inches of her own death), but in some cases the disclosure is extraordinary. One person on a course run by one of the authors disclosed in full detail the day he discovered that he had a serious cancer and, indeed, even at the time he was on the course his survival prognosis was unfavourable beyond a short period of years. We have also heard of one woman, not on a course of our own, disclosing, apparently for the first time, an abortion she had never felt able to confide to anyone else.

It is not, of course, the material being revealed which is important in this session. It is the vulnerability of allowing others to share a secret part of yourself which begins a process of bonding. The first step towards real friendship is to exchange and share vulnerabilities. The process is not designed to create in someone a weakness which others can sympathise with; the vulnerability is vulnerability in *oneself*. The honesty with which someone gives a part of themselves to others is very apparent to others, and it creates in people a willingness to respond in like manner. It is what the person gives which is important, not what they receive; they give away certain barriers to friendship and inevitably they find that they lose a part of their fear. Most barriers are created as a fear against the disapproval of others yet, when brought down in an atmosphere of honesty, few people will take advantage of such openness. Those who do try to gain advantage would incur the disapproval of others and indeed would recognise an unsatisfactory part of their own character which would itself be a barrier broken down.

Your best moment

Just as above, each participant is asked to disclose their best or most exciting moment, or achievement, in their life. The process is very similar and again it is the person's own feelings towards their disclosure which is important, rather than the feelings of the audience. It is actually very difficult to describe a good moment without perhaps unreasonable pride or boasting, and indeed it cannot easily be done except between those who have trust with each other; friends, for example, can talk about achievements without embarrassing each other, whereas a certain modesty might set in among less closely associated people. The idea of this part of the session is to encourage using the trust which is building up from earlier sessions to teach the person how to disclose their own greatest moments without the need for boasting and bragging. In fact this is often harder than revealing your worst moment and many participants learn more about themselves from this than before. As a general rule, during such sessions there is a great deal of camaraderie building up with much humour between participants and this becomes one of the first drivers towards friendship.

The magic chair

Each member of the team sits in 'the magic chair' facing all the other members who are arranged in a semi-circle around the front of it. The team members are then told to give whatever praise they can to the person in the magic chair. They cannot be critical, only praising. They can comment on how good looking a person is, how intelligent they have found them to be, how well dressed they are or indeed on any other positive aspect of the person which they believe to be true. The rule is that the praise must be honest.

Following this session the person in the magic chair is asked to say how they felt about the praise they were receiving.

The results of this are revealing; in business, particularly, people are so often on the receiving end of false praise that they find genuine praise hard to accept. Given that communication is 20 per cent verbal and 80 per cent non-verbal, they have usually been able to detect the falseness for what it was, but such falseness often becomes almost a norm.

In the magic chair they have to face praise which they know is genuine and it is remarkable how barriers break down as a person begins to lose the fear of being falsely praised and accepts the pleasure of praise for its own sake. When relating their own feelings back to the group people will often comment that: 'While I was doing that I learned a lot about myself' or something similar, and will often go on to say that after one or two such sessions they are able to accept the praise without feeling embarrassed and indeed to give praise without feeling embarrassed, which is itself equally difficult.

Make a positive statement

Each person is asked to stand in front of the whole group and make a dramatic and positive statement about themselves. The statement should be verbal as well as non-verbal, and for example can be the very loud declaration, 'I am a fantastic salesman' or 'I am going to make my next assignment extraordinary'. In each case they might accompany their statement by a gesture such as throwing the hands wide and throwing the head back and so on.

This is not the way that we normally act, though it is sometimes the way we feel. Actually to display an inner feeling in front of others is again a willingness to share a perceived vulnerability and it will be reciprocated.

Perform a play

One other technique we use, though usually in more advanced teambuilding courses, is to make the object of the exercise to get the team in syndicates to put together a five-minute performance of theatre and deliver it with passion to an audience, i.e. the rest of the team. (For small groups the use of a video is essential.) In this instance the facilitator autocratically gives a syndicate group the title of the play to be performed which can be as abstract as 'Being an orchard' or as concrete as 'The D-Day landings'. People need only to see that instant teambuilding is possible, and that it can be dramatically effective for them to take those lessons to heart and apply them with permanence.

Tongue twisters

Each person is given a sheet of three of four tongue twisters which they have to say out loud to the other members of the group. This usually creates considerable humour and camaraderie, which is an essential part of breaking down barriers between people. As an added refinement the team leader or facilitator can ask the individual to deliver a particular tongue twister in a variety of strange voices just to add to the humour. Learning to laugh *with* one another – rather than *at* one another – is a basic trust-building exercise and it is very easily achievable through this method.

These techniques work! Over a period of time we began to find that the commitment to the process was demonstrably stronger than some of the skills-based courses we were running. At the present time we are continuing to develop these techniques for a City-based financial institution and also for a customer-oriented commercial company building on the work they have done in heavy industry. Arising from this, course delegates have demanded follow-up courses in the same teams. This did not surprise us as we had realised from other such courses that people felt unsated, and indeed unhappy, that the course was over. This was not only due to the subject matter and the interaction that had been created, but also that people had forged friendships, i.e. they had in fact become a working team. The lesson to be drawn, which can only be learnt by time and experience, is that such people will now be very much more confident in forming teams with other people, and will indeed find themselves acting as a facilitator and introducing to their teams some of the non-business teambuilding attributes that we have related above.

One last warning. The old cliché about avoiding sex, religion and politics as topics of disclosure is valid here; they are topics where discussion of the subject matter will often replace the process. They are also the three subjects where overt or covert criticism is often difficult. Almost any other subject seems able to be applied without such controversy between people. The very skilled trainer might well want deliberately to introduce one of these three, but to the less experienced trainer it is dangerous and the rewards are rarely worth the extra effort involved.

9. TEAM COMMUNICATIONS

'I know you believe you understand what you think I said, but I am not sure if you realise that what you heard is not what I meant.'

Anon

In the 1980s one of the authors was working in the North Sea on an oil platform 200 miles north of Aberdeen. One of the stories going the rounds was told about communications, by the team leader of a drilling crew. Drilling crews are highly motivated teams who pitch their skills against weather and geology. They demonstrate high task attainment and have great team pride in getting the best job done. In this particular story the drilling crew were pushing as much pipe as possible into the North Sea bed. A part of the machinery broke and there was no spare in the stores, meaning that the drilling operation had to be suspended. The problem was reported to the off-shore installation manager, the 'boss' of the platform. Immediately, he, using his satellite link, located a spare part in one of the firm's warehouses in Louisiana, USA. A jet was chartered to fly the spare part to New York where another plane was chartered to fly the part to Aberdeen. At Aberdeen Airport the machine part was helicoptered to the oil platform. The whole operation was concluded in less than twenty-four hours and the off-shore manager congratulated himself on the communications systems and quick response that had enabled the drilling to resume so quickly. Three days later, after the crew change, he learned that such a spare part was held in the warehouse in Aberdeen. Thousands of pounds had been wasted on what appeared at first to be good information flow and communications.

Endless books are written, articles appear every day, lectures, seminars and management games are conducted by business managers in communications, but we still cannot get it right. So what, we may well ask, is going wrong? We have the information technology systems for quick response communications literally at our fingertips. These systems seem to work even during the most difficult conditions. During the Gulf War we were still receiving telephone messages from occupied Kuwait, while having our information flow restricted by our own government for security reasons. The issue here is that although we are good at creating technical communication systems and training people how to use them, we are not so good at understanding what information we need to do the task. We normally only train people how to use the modern technology and not how to apply it. We have often seen the innocent misapplication of modern information technology due to lack of planning and thought about the problem, and by far the most common is the use of electronic mail systems. Electronic mail packages are being installed daily into businesses with only functional training, i.e. how to use the system with no training on how to be on the receiving end of the system. One harassed middle manager confided that he was frightened to go on holiday, because when he comes back his terminal is stuffed full of 'E' mail which takes him weeks to deal with, not including the gratuitous nonsense messages that seem to amuse so much of British management.

> '"Out of sight, out of mind" when translated into Russian
> [by computer] and then back again into English, became
> "Invisible Maniac"'
>
> Arthur Calder-Marshall

In order for the team to function effectively it must receive fast and accurate information that it can believe in, and take action upon. In many organisations, however, we are castrating management by information overload. The maxim that the more information, the less likelihood of a quick, or indeed any, decision is true. Any manager will tell you stories of decisions made with very little information that often achieve the greatest impact on the organisation, because in this instance the manager must use management and entrepreneurial flair, rather than ploughing through trees and trees of computer printout of facts, probabilities, variance etc. If we consider this information overload in terms of team work we can easily see that if we give the team too much information to digest then two things can happen.

First, the team will spend most of its useful time in sifting through the information, asking for clarifications and supporting facts, evidence and calling for rechecking of information which means that most, if not all, of the team's effort will be put into the interpretation, filtering and reporting of the data.

Secondly, the team will defuse the very synergy and radical thinking that it was formed for in the first place. Simply put, the members of the team will be crushed by the information and will become super-careful in the decision-making process.

What, then, can the team leader do to assist the team in its ability to handle information and make best use of it? First we must go back to basics and agree our thoughts on what we mean by information flow and communications.

Most of our organisations are structured along military lines with the chief at the top and the braves at the bottom. The reasons for this historically are that when businesses were being formed the only structure that people could observe and copy was the Roman Catholic church and they had borrowed their structure from the organisation of the Roman Legion. The need for control, order and discipline led organisations to adopt military-style communication systems. The general gives the order and the troops advance. This vertical method of communication is still in existence in too many of our companies. Tom Peters, in *Thriving on Chaos*, argues very strongly that we must encourage horizontal communications as well. The horizontal and vertical information flow and communications must be free and unrestricted. But how can we achieve this? In our experience this can only be brought about by a total culture change in the organisation in general, and towards the communication systems in the specific.

To our mind successful organisations need successful communications, and they in turn need a culture to nurture and build on the present systems. So, are there any universal rules that can be adopted by businesses wishing to improve the information flow and communications within and across teams in the organisation? Probably not, but in our experience certain aspects of behaviour must be visible in order to achieve the degree of maturity of communications necessary to run our businesses in an increasingly chaotic world.

- The team leader must have a reputation for honesty and integrity in his or her dealings with the team and third parties.
- The team leader must be given by management clear and easily communicable statements of requirements concerning the task, as well as the reasons why.
- The team must understand the present systems in the organisation and the degree of reliability that they can place on them, so that they can monitor information flows around the shortfalls.
- The team with its team leader must establish respect and trust with the other teams in the organisation, so that energies are concentrated on problems and not on scoring points off each other.
- The teams must at all times practise professionalism, and the high duty of care that is needed when dealing with other teams in the organisation. Professionalism also demands assertion in attitudes and availability of information.
- The teams should adopt Tom Peters's idea of management by walking about (MBWA). The increase in *ad hoc* information flows and establishing informal lines of communication are enhanced through the mobility of teams and team leaders. This can also lead to the setting up of informal networking information flows.

Management must treat staff and the workforce as mature and responsible, and able to take the bad news as well as the good news. We must, at all levels of the organisation, train and encourage our teams to handle and access communication, and we must empower all of us to seek and find the information necessary to do the job.

In one of the organisations that we work with, an enlightened manager has introduced boasting sessions for team leaders. In front of all departmental staff, team leaders have to stand up and boast for five minutes with all the successes and positive things that his or her team has done since the last session. This excellent example of horizontal communications may be too un-British for many people, but it works, and once the shyness has been overcome the team leaders look forward to singing the praises of their team and improving communications in that department.

Before team leaders engage in communication with their teams they should review six key questions.

- What do I intend to say or write?
- What will I actually say or write, sometimes in spite of my good intentions?
- What will I really mean? (What will be the emotional impact of what I say or write?)
- What does my team expect to hear or read?
- What will the individual team members actually read or hear, despite what is said or written at times?
- How will the team feel about what they read or hear?

The team leader's task is therefore threefold:

1. to translate what is significant to him or her so that it will be acceptable to the team; if it is not acceptable, the communication will be rejected;
2. to translate what is important to him or her so that it is meaningful to the team, on their terms rather than those of the sender;
3. to translate what is significant to the sender into terms that will have the impact sought on the team.

It must therefore be borne in mind that the team must dictate the manner of communication to which it will respond positively.

The team must also determine the quantity and quality of the information, as well as the manner of communication. It is far too simplistic for team leaders to talk about scoping the job (i.e. taking an all-embracing view of the job) and determining the information required. If you pre-determine the information, then the only decisions that the team will be able to make will be based on the information that the team called for. If we take the opposite extreme and allow the team to be bombarded with unlimited information then, as we have already argued, the team cannot function effectively.

Is there a pragmatic compromise then? In our experience, probably no, because only half the right information is worse than the two scenarios painted above. We do not claim to have a solution, but we can approach the problem from a different angle.

Nearly all the information received by the team is in written form and in turn the team turns out information in a similar manner. Why do we not turn our attention from written to verbal communications, perhaps supported by visual aids, which at least has the advantage of being able to question the presenter.

A few years ago as a consultant one of us sat through an extremely boring post-mortem concerning an engineering fault. During the presentation by a senior professional engineer copies were given to us of drawings of the situation before and after the fracture of a piece of machinery. The in-house drawing office had done a superb job and everyone except two of us were totally impressed. Seeing the frown on our faces we were invited to make any comments, to which we replied, 'Wouldn't a few Polaroid pictures have given us a better visual image of what had happened?'.

In another place a senior manager of a large industrial site in the north of England is trying to bring MBWA back to his plant. He is insisting that all his team leaders 'walk their patch' at least once a day to see what is going on rather than calling for information from his subordinates either in written or verbal form.

The communications systems in an organisation are therefore not to be cemented in stone. The team leader with the team must determine what suits and on what particular occasion. The senior personnel manager who replaces written monthly reports with five-minute presentations from senior staff has a better understanding of the issues, as he or she can more readily see the degree of commitment and prioritisation through body language, than by the cold written word.

Another interesting observation of team development that we have made is when the team gets stuck over certain problems, and it starts seeking and demanding much more information. The abilities of teams to solve problems are often, as we have argued, in inverse proportion to the amount of information needed to do so.

A few years ago one of the authors was working in the head office of a national chain of retail jewellers. The chief buyer then was a manager of the old school who, being computer illiterate, was forever bemoaning the volume and complexity of his printed-out stock records. He had not learned to cull the information to suit himself and his team of buyers. One particular example shows this: every month at his stock review meeting he would religiously point out in a mournful voice that there had been no movement on the number of silver figures of the Pope left over from the Pope's one and only visit to the UK. He was not willing to melt them down for scrap value thereby incurring a loss, but in these circumstances an overall value would have been sufficient, as opposed to the numbers of items in every one of his outlets.

The team must therefore be trained and encouraged to use all their senses for receiving and sending out information. Team members must practise MBWA and learn to report back verbally as well as in written form. Where large amounts of complex data have to be digested, tasks in communication should be delegated to the individual team member best suited to deal with it. This person can then brief the team on the results and be questioned on the findings.

The team leader has a responsibility to ensure that communication in the team is effective; there are times, however, when team leaders seem to show just the wrong initiative. So, for those less-than-enlightened leaders we offer the following guidelines to stifling communication (enlightened team leaders will know how to bend these rules!).

Guidelines to stifling communication

1. Do **NOT** adhere to the KISS principle (Keep it simple, stupid).

2. **USE** the language of lawyers and bureaucrats.

3. **ONLY** communicate vertically, up the line.

4. **ONLY** communicate facts, never opinions.

5. **ONLY** communicate good news and remember to grab all the credit that's going.

6. **DELEGATE** the communication of bad news.

7. **WHERE POSSIBLE** communicate by letter, memos and so on; **NEVER** verbally unless you really have to.

8. **DO NOT** allocate a specific time for team briefings.

9. **DISCOURAGE** verbal comprehension by belittling the questioner.

10. **TREAT** team members as immature in any communications with them (make some time to practise talking down to people!).

11. **ALWAYS** use politics as an excuse for not being open and honest with your team.

12. **RIDICULE** new ideas from below and treat them with suspicion.

13. **CRITICISE** freely and withhold recognition and praise.

14. **REGARD** all problems as failure, and discourage people drawing problems to your attention.

15. **USING** IT (information technology) systems, restrict information flows with hierarchical passwords.

16. **REGARD** open communications by management down the line as a dismissible offence.

17. **TAKE EVERY OPPORTUNITY** you can to distance yourself from company initiatives, especially those to do with communications.

18. **RE-STATE** the company rules as often as possible, using the company notice boards.

19. **ASK** departments and teams to challenge and criticise each other's proposals.

20. **IN MEETINGS**, always encourage in-fighting and praise the winner.

10. TRAINING MAINTENANCE

'Training is a journey, not a destination.'

In order that teams maintain their effectiveness throughout the period of their existence, either of short or long duration, there must be continuous training available to the members, keeping them up to date at all times. Where teams have long or permanent lives, then there will be personnel changes periodically and there must be adequate structured training to ensure that the right people are available at the right time. This chapter sets out the requirements of a proper programme of training maintenance.

Training is a journey, not a destination, and if management would adopt this simple philosophy then the short-termism of the training in most organisations could be resisted. In most UK companies that we have worked in, training is either regarded as interventionalist – to correct a perceived need – or, funds permitting, a napalm approach is taken, where everyone is trained irrespective of training or personal development needs. Training is nearly always implemented post-promotion and for this reason team development is often held up while the training needs are put in place.

It is widely acknowledged by most organisations that people are the prime asset, and if other valuable assets need maintenance, then so do employees. In our experience we have found that senior managers have little interest in training and do not regard it as a strategic investment. Senior managers have scant knowledge of their own organisation's training needs and do not know how their training courses compare with those of their competitors at home or overseas.

Training can be compartmentalised, but whether it is called

133

skills training, technology training or management training, it should all have the same goal. Training equips all employees to perform competently in their present and future jobs, increasing the organisation's effectiveness and individual job satisfaction. Line-management must realise that training and personal development helps drive the business and they must accept responsibility for implementation, identification of needs, and development of people through training courses.

The first stage of establishing a training maintenance pro-gramme is for the team leader with the team to construct a simple skill matrix of the skills necessary to do the tasks, including potential future projects that may be given to, or won by, the team. It is essential for the team leader to involve all the team members at this point, so that they can openly offer strengths and weaknesses to the group.

Having established the ideal profile, the second stage is to overlay on the matrix what the team feel they can now offer. This will show up surplus as well as gaps in the skills needed to complete the projects. At this point it may be necessary through the training department or personnel department to seek and find the missing skills to plug the gaps on a secondment or co-option basis, at least until the team's training needs have been met and the individuals in the team feel confident in the new areas. We have found that the proper use of secondees to teams is to make them in-house trainers during their stay.

The third stage in establishing the training needs of a team is the needs assessment survey which should be conducted by the team leader in individual sessions with the team members. Privacy and confidentiality are of the utmost importance, as many potentially embarrassing matters may be uncovered. The team leader may find that some of the team cannot read or write to the level necessary for the communications needed by the team. Other issues that may be made visible are computer illiteracy, numeracy, as well as core skills' weaknesses in their own field of expertise. The team leader will then need to draw up a team profile which will compare against the team members' current strengths and weaknesses in key areas.

These can then be discussed with the in-house training pro-fessionals and/or line management, or with outside agents such as consultants, colleges, schools etc. The training experts will then be able to advise the team leader what courses are on offer, both for in-house and external application.

Before we move on, let us recap on what we are suggesting that the team leader does. The leader has scoped the potential and current workload of the team to establish what skills are necessary to do the job in the most effective manner. He or she has done this with the full participation of the team. They have then, as a team, established what they feel competent to do, and this has then been compared with what is needed, and surplus and gaps in skills have been identified. They have decided to plug the gaps with secondees or have co-opted people where necessary, so that the team can effectively function, and at the same time the team has established its own training needs so that secondees and co-optees can be released at the earliest opportunity. At all levels of the process this has been made a team task. The only individual consultations were to look more closely at individual and personal training needs. We have then suggested that the team leader should examine the internal and external training available to the team. The team leader, subject to budgetary constraint, can then execute the training plan.

We will now look at this plan of action in more detail and discuss some of the problems that team leaders may well encounter.

Scoping the work

A team is formed for a specific set of tasks and purposes, and the first action is to hold a brainstorming session to draw out all the elements necessary to fulfil the project. From the brainstorming exercise we can establish the tasks to be done and the skills necessary to do the work.

At this juncture the team can also agree on the tools to do the job, and list the equipment and the other resources necessary that will instil ownership of the problem. The scope is now an outline plan; it is not fixed but is a flexible approach for the next stage.

Team self-assessment

Another brainstorming session is now necessary to establish what the team feels competent to do and there the team leader will need all his or her leadership skills to get over the hump of enthusiasm. Because stage one has quite rightly instilled an immediate sense of ownership, the team will close ranks and quickly decide that it has more skills than it is capable of demonstrating. The team leader's job is to tease out through challenge that the team does not possess all these skills, and that they must honestly state their limitations and also what they will potentially feel uncomfortable with.

Team task and skills matching

The team leader can now hold a more formal team meeting to compare the needs of the task with the availability of skills of the team. This will throw up surpluses and gaps. It is the gaps that we are interested in. From our experience at this stage the team will try and rationalise the gaps, and some individuals – in order to protect the team from outsiders – will say that although they haven't got a particular skill they can quickly learn it, and will begin to offer individual commitments. The team leader must resist these offers and steer the team to the realisation that it is not to the discredit of the team to acknowledge skills gaps, and indeed regard them as opportunities to strengthen the team with the necessary 'experts'. The team will accept this so long as it is understood, i.e. made part of the team contract, that secondees and co-optees are invited in not only to plug the gaps but also to train the team. In some very self-protective teams it may be necessary to put a time ruling on how long these sub-team members will be with the team.

In fact, in our experience, secondees often become accepted as part of the team in a very short period of time.

Individual needs assessment survey

This is the most difficult part of the exercise for the team leader, as we now need to establish the strengths and weaknesses of the individual team players. In our experience this must be done by the team leader and not delegated to the personnel or training departments. Needs assessment survey forms are legion and in our experience the best form is one devised by the team leader in consultation with the team.

(The outline needs assessment survey form set out on pages 138–139 is used by the authors as a model which is then tailored to the needs of a particular team.)

The team leader's job then, with empathy, is to establish with the individual team members the training needs to enable the members to participate fully. This diagnostic work can be likened to that of a general practitioner in consultation with a patient who then, with mutual agreement, refers that person to the consultant. Interestingly enough, senior managers are often shy in these situations and it does take considerable teambuilding skills to get them to admit to weaknesses.

The training experts

The team leader will then have a shopping list of training needs, including his or her own, that can then be discussed with the in-house training experts. The problem we have found here is that in most organisations the training experts are in fact training administrators, and not up-front trainers. They are very good at information on what courses are on offer, both internally and externally, but often have scarce knowledge of how to design a training course, nor indeed whether the courses on offer actually fit the bill.

In one training department we worked in, many external courses were on offer. When the training expert was challenged by us on course content, he actually stated that the content was somewhat irrelevant, and that by sending 'Fred' on this course, he would meet other people from other organisations, which he felt was the real value of training. Team leaders must resist such ideas!

If, and such a situation will arise, there are no internal or external courses on offer that really suit, you may have to call in external training consultants to design a course for your needs, or alternatively have a go at it yourself, before handing it to a third party. Your design may be a bit crude and may lack the fancy language now adopted by trainers, but it will state the requirements clearly for an outside agent.

138

Needs assessment survey form

NAME _____

DEPT/WORKSHOP _____

AGE _____ QUALIFICATIONS _____

_____

_____

1. List courses currently booked.

TITLE _____ DATE _____

TITLE _____ DATE _____

TITLE _____ DATE _____

2. List courses currently being undertaken.

TITLE _____ DATE _____

TITLE _____ DATE _____

3. List internal company courses attended.

TITLE _____ DATE _____

TITLE _____ DATE _____

TITLE _____ DATE _____

4. List external courses attended.

TITLE _____ DATE _____

TITLE _____ DATE _____

5. List management courses recommended by line manager.

TITLE _____ DATE _____

TITLE _____ DATE _____

6. List skills courses recommended by line-manager.

TITLE _____ DATE _____

7. What courses do you wish to attend in respect of skills training?

TITLE _____ DATE _____

TITLE _____ DATE _____

8. What courses do you wish to attend in respect of management training?

TITLE _____ DATE _____

TITLE _____ DATE _____

9. What courses do you wish to attend for personal development?

TITLE _____ DATE _____

TITLE _____ DATE _____

10. What, if anything, are you currently studying for?

TITLE _____ DATE _____

TITLE _____ DATE _____

11. What internal company courses not yet attended are you aware of?

TITLE _____ DATE _____

TITLE _____ DATE _____

TITLE _____ DATE _____

12. What external courses funded by the company are you aware of?

TITLE _____ DATE _____

TITLE _____ DATE _____

13. List your priorities for courses, (not your preferences).

_____

_____

14. Now list your personal preferences for courses to attend.

_____

_____

15. What (if any) other training do you feel you need, and why?

_____

_____

16. What areas do you feel particularly strong in?

_____

17. What areas do you feel particularly weak in?

_____

Execution of the training needs

The team leader will now have to put into execution the training of the team members. There is an increasing tendency to do this all too quickly. Most people have learned by rote, therefore they want to continue to do so, and this will take time. Also, the team leader must keep in mind the problem of 'learning overload'. Most of us leave school, college etc. at say sixteen, eighteen or twenty-one years of age and often that is the last formal training we will undertake, apart from the odd course here and there. From our experience good courses with a balance between content and process, i.e. theory supplemented with games, exercises and discussion, should be of one to three days' duration at the most. We prefer two-day courses with which delegates and companies seem comfortable. We are reminded of Winston Churchill's comment, 'Personally, I'm always ready to learn, although I do not always like being taught.'

Team leaders must recognise that training maintenance is the life blood of the team. This is of equal importance both to short and long duration teams. Short-term teams may be dissolved after an agreed period of time, but the people do not dissolve. The individuals will be formed into new teams and every new skill acquired will be an added value to the new team. With longer-term teams who, in our experience, resist training needs the most, it is important that continuous training is undertaken not just for the sake of using up a training budget, but dedicated training in technology, management skills, corporate issues, so that they can adapt to the new key issues facing the organisation as opposed to a historical re-run of the old ways.

Team training is an investment for the future and is an integral part of the teambuilding process.

Training maintenance – teamleader checklist

- Training is a journey, not a destination.
- Training should not be a stop–go policy.
- People are the major fixed assets of an organisation and as such need regular maintenance.
- Training is a strategic investment.

- We cannot rely any longer on poaching staff to fill skills shortages.
- Training is a function and the responsibility of line-management.
- Training should be in anticipation of promotion, not a reward for promotion.
- There are three major training needs for the individual; skills, management, personal. Do not forget the last one.
- Compile a task and skill matrix of your team.
- Conduct, update and use your training needs assessment survey information.

Choosing external trainers

Large organisations will have their own training departments with networks built between themselves and the local colleges, and industrial and professional organisations. The problem for the smaller organisations is where and who to choose for advice and help, as and when needed. The following list is not exhaustive, but will help line-management to decide who to turn to.

1. Every industry has its own trade association etc. and these are readily documented in trade magazines, i.e. the Chemical Industries Association (CIA).
2. Professional associations, i.e. the Institute of Chartered Accountants, are always willing to give advice on training through their members.
3. Business schools, universities, polytechnics etc. These academic institutions obviously have dedicated departments or faculties readily available for local business. Most have now developed partnerships with government and local industries.
4. Specialist training consultants, such as the company run by the authors of this book – APW Training. These bring together academic and practical experience from many fields.

11. MOTIVATING THE INDIVIDUAL

'To business that we love we rise betime, And go to't with delight.'

William Shakespeare

Motivation is a separate subject in its own right and many books have been written on it. We have concentrated on those aspects relevant to team building, team members and team leaders in this chapter, and we have drawn from our practical experience of teambuilding in many organisations.

One of the team leader's roles is to motivate the team, and in order to do so he or she must understand how and why people are motivated as individuals, as well as in teams. We know that motivation can be brought about in a variety of ways and the team leader may have to experiment to get the most effective formula for the group. Historically, motivation must have existed since the dawn of man. It has, of course, taken on different forms in differing societies and situations. Presumaby our earliest ancestors were self-motivating; creating fire from their need for warmth, and manipulating tools and weapons in their need for survival. Those who were less motivated or whose motivations developed in different ways would have fallen by the wayside in the competition against those whose motivations were in tune with the needs of the time.

First, let us refresh our memories of pre-scientific motivation techniques, so-called because they were in place before the writings of Frederick Taylor, the father of scientific management. They were simplistic, but often very successful; however, they are no longer socially acceptable in a modern industrialised society. Those pre-scientific methods were coercion, conniving,

142

compensation, 'cuddle and coddle' and – most powerfully – fear. It must be admitted that they still operate in many of our smaller organisations.

Motivation by fear

One of the most obvious forms of motivation is fear. Fear can be exercised in many subtle ways from rumour to naked aggression. We learn in early history that by using whips and starvation you could get the pyramids built; it is a powerful tool that, if it cannot move the mountain, can at least let you build one of your own.

> In the James Bond film, *Live and Let Die*, a humorous and memorable example of fear motivation is given. In one scene Agent 007 is being pursued by a group of gangsters out to prevent him drawing a halt to their activities. Over the radio their leader announces to the group, 'The man that gets him stays alive'.

The modern equivalents of fear strategy are threats of redundancy, being moved to a different area, change of job status and so on.

There is no doubt that in the very short run fear is a good motivator, but the people subjected to such a strategy will, eventually, want revenge, often in the form of leaving the organisation or, at the least, just functioning at the minimum level to remain in the organisation.

Coercion

Coercion can be regarded as a modified form of threat and fear using authority as a means of motivation. At its simplest, when the chair (chairman or woman) of the company asks you to do something it carries with it a greater implication of perceived threat than when your line-manager tells you to do that same something. In practical terms – often depending on your position in the 'pecking order' – the chair may have less influence, or at least use that influence less against you, than your own reporting manager would. Whether it is fair to regard coercion as a motivational tool will often depend on the organisation, and that in turn is dependent upon the history of the organisation and how it has coerced people in the past.

> One very popular story in the City is told of the chairman of a large organisation who had banned smoking in his building. One morning on entering the lift he observed a young man smoking, and in the lift with him were two very senior members of his staff. The chairman asked the young man how much he earned a week. The young man replied £180, whereupon from a large wad of money the chairman peeled off £180 and gave it to the young man with the words, 'You're fired, go and collect your cards'. The young man said nothing and as a dutiful courier, delivered the package he had come to deliver and went back to his own firm with no doubt the largest tip of the day.

Manipulation

Motivation can often be achieved by manipulation. Manipulation consists of manoeuvring a person into a set of circumstances where they feel that their best course of action is to act as you have intimated you wish them to act. Manipulation is not designed so that the person being manipulated feels that they are achieving any goals of their own; usually the best they can hope for is that they are not placed in a disadvantageous position by non-compliance. One of the most common forms of manipulation exercised by organisations is when the company (without any undue pressure) offers promotion through a job move to a different location, and at the same time hints that in this organisation promotion is only offered once by this route, and if you turn it down you will not be offered it again.

One of the authors interviewed a senior employee of one of the major high street banks; under forty years old, he had a comfortable life that he was quite happy with working in a major UK city. It had been indicated to him that he might have to be posted to the Far East, which he very clearly did not want. However, the point had apparently been made clear that if the position was not accepted then he might as well regard himself as having reached the limit of his promotion prospects! (Often cynically referred to in personnel files as 'This person is ideally suited to his present position'.)

Positive motivation techniques

Up to this point people are being motivated by various forms of fear, and they are acting in a way indicated because they feel that any other course is detrimental to them.

We can now look at more positive motivation techniques where, by their correct application, people will act in the way you want them to because they believe it actually achieves goals of their own. The first of these is compensation, and using money as the prime motivator. A naïve interpretation of motivation is that people can only be motivated by money. In other words, if a person is paid more they will perform better. This is hopelessly wrong, though it is true that if a person is not paid what they perceive themselves to be worth, then they will not feel motivated. Money therefore is not a motivator in itself, but its absence is a de-motivator. However, once people recognise they are being paid a reasonable wage then motivation ceases if other goals are not being met. If a person does not feel that their work is of value, that their work is appreciated or that their work is making a significant contribution to the team effort, then no amount of money will motivate them.

Indeed, such an attitude on the part of management can be dangerous; if people perceive that they are being overpaid to 'buy' them in some way they become resentful and angry. Often their personal circumstances do not easily lead them to give up their job and they become locked in a de-motivated cycle that is not beneficial to themselves or to their company.

In the 'cuddle and coddle' school of motivation the organisation seeks to provide its staff with fair wages, superior fringe benefits and excellent working conditions in order that they feel grateful. From our experience of working in these types of organisations the management are normally paternalistic, often referring to the workforce as 'lads' or 'our lads' , and always reminding them how grateful they should feel. When the gratitude is not forthcoming time-worn motivational phrases such as, 'If you don't like working here there's the gate' arise. What we are seeing now, however, is a breakdown of the cuddle and cod-dle system. Because of the economic climate during recessions, many organisations have taken the opportunity to halt or even withdraw superior fringe benefits, and we have seen the government seemingly determined to tax such perks out of existence and steer us towards the US system of higher wages and no fringe benefits. Recently, working in an organisation that has withdrawn nearly 50 per cent of its fringe benefits, the staff were stating how de-motivated they were, but as we pointed out through team discussions they were confusing morale with motivation and morale is as changeable as the weather. We concluded that cuddle and coddle strategies no doubt attract people into organisations, but in themselves they are not motivational.

Working with companies in the late 1970s and 1980s, it was becoming obvious that pre-scientific motivation techniques were being challenged and human resource departments were putting in place more enlightened and progressive methods of motivating people with the introduction of clearer grading systems, wider share ownership schemes, more open and frank appraisal systems, and better training and retraining. Unfortunately – but perhaps not surprisingly – the 1990s is seeing a fast return to the old motivation techniques, and it would seem that some senior managers openly welcome the opportunity to apply pressure on the workforce to achieve the organisation's objectives. Fear of redundancy and mobility are now motivating many people not to challenge our organisations and systems, which in the long run will lead to inefficiency and the continuance of bad working methods. It is all the more depressing to see a household name dismissing its entire workforce as a legal let out to introduce a pay freeze. The word survival is now the modern equivalent of fear strategies.

It is therefore all the more refreshing to see that even in today's climate some progressive leaders are pushing ahead with cultural change as a path to motivation, while at the same time developing quality and customer focus initiatives. (Both of these topics are examined elsewhere in the book.)

In conclusion then, money is not the only motivator and if used as a reward it becomes a norm and increased supplies of money are then required to achieve the same level of activity or commit-ment, until overload and resentment are reached.

Sometimes even rewards that seem more enlightened can be counter-productive. Share ownership is a modern reward given by some companies, but it can be de-motivating if the share prices fall, and we have all seen how volatile the shares market can be. In effect, employees then discover they are not only sharing in the profits or at least the growth of the company, but also in its losses or recessions.

No work on teambuilding can ignore the behavioural scientists and we must ask whether they have any relevance in the corporate life of the 1990s. Some of the behaviouralists and their work have gone out of fashion and others are being reassessed in the light of total quality management and managing change programmes. The team leader, and indeed members of the team, will understand that each individual has a differing set of past experiences and the person's own perception of those experiences will affect his or her beliefs about the world around them, about other people and about themselves. For example, the young toddler who pulls himself up to a standing position using the radiator becomes confused when a week later the radiator, now turned on, burns him; he therefore avoids radiators until he is taught or discovers for himself how to approach them with caution. Similarly, motivation is based on a wide range of past experiences and beliefs about the individual, the organisation and society.

In turn the organisation arranges its work and policies based on its beliefs about individuals and behaviour. Organisations, if they are to survive and grow, must change their behaviour, which in turn means that the individuals in the organisation must also learn to act in a different way.

One of the most popular, or at least well-known, writers on motivation is Douglas McGregor, who in his book *The Human Side of Enterprise*, debated that managers' behaviour towards the workforce is very much influenced by some basic assumptions which he separated into his Theory X and Theory Y. In contemporary management thinking we can liken Theory X to the traditional control strategies and Theory Y to a more enlightened and empowering system. Perhaps because the two theories are listing the extremes of our views of human behaviour at work, and perhaps also because it is understandable and relevant today, people still openly debate these theories.

Theory X is based on the belief that by nature the typical

147

worker is lazy, doesn't like work, is unambitious at work, will avoid responsibility, is passive, must be punished and rewarded, needs tight supervision and is incapable of self-discipline.

Theory Y, on the other hand, states that to the average worker work is as natural as play, work can be satisfying or punishing depending on circumstances, and people are capable of taking responsibility. Indeed, under the right conditions, people actually seek responsibility. Motivation does not involve what the manager does to individuals – the motivating forces already exist in the workforce. Ingenuity and creativity do not only exist at the managerial level.

We have already stated that team leaders have a responsibility to motivate the team. Team leaders will, however, have an inclination towards either Theory X or Theory Y, depending upon their own past experiences and the types of organisations they have worked in. If a person joins the organisation at sixteen, eighteen or twenty-one years old and stays put in that business, then their beliefs about the workforce will eventually be shaped by that firm. Conversely, a team leader who moves from one organisation to another will be in a position to compare and reassess opinions and views held, in the realisation that he or she feels or felt uncomfortable in some situations. Problems may arise when we find a Theory Y oriented team leader having to manage people through Theory X systems.

From our experience in the front line of industry and commerce, what has now developed is Theory Y oriented senior management, staff who want to be treated in a Theory Y manner, but being led and managed by Theory X middle management. The reason we have found for middle management to adopt Theory X is because they are having to operate the organisation on codes of practice and work systems developed and enhanced in an environment with Theory X leanings. There is no doubt that at first sight Theory Y is seductive, is attractive and no doubt the modern team leader would prefer to live in that society, but Theory Y cannot become the norm unless we are prepared to introduce more Theory Y systems and procedures into our organisations.

A closer look at the needs of the individual was developed by psychologist Abraham Maslow and most managers will have heard of Maslow's hierarchy of needs. Maslow contended that for the human individual at work, certain needs had to be satisfied before they could move on to the next set of higher level needs.

Maslow's hierarchy can be displayed in this diagram:

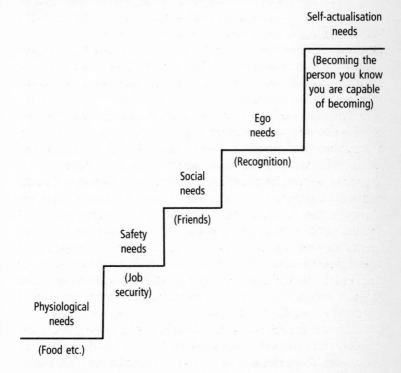

Maslow's first needs were physiological, these are the lower level needs and the most basic; for example, food, drink, shelter and rest. In the developed world the majority of people find these needs satisfied through our remuneration systems. The second group of needs to be satisfied are safety needs, i.e. the need for protection against danger or deprivation, including job security. Once these needs were fulfilled people would aspire to the social needs, i.e. the need to work in teams, and forming friendships at work. Once these needs were fulfilled then the higher level needs could be sought; these are recognition by the organisation and self-esteem needs, self-confidence and seeking knowledge. If the above needs are satisfied, and in our experience this is rare, then in Maslow's definition we can aspire to self-actualisation needs.

This is the need we all have to become the person we believe we have the potential to become.

Maslow's hierarchy is useful to the team leader in identifying the stages people have to go through before they can give their full potential to the organisation, as well as highlighting blockages in the systems that are stopping people. A recent problem that has arisen here is that in the last few years we have been taking away Maslow's second need, i.e. the need for job security. Job security is now much less common in our organisations and many firms for reasons of cyclical trading have replaced full-time employees with contractors (often ex-employees). Contractors have very little job security and consequently form fewer friendships and other social affiliations at work.

The long-term effect of living in a work environment that is less secure than before is still under debate, but we have increasingly seen that the social needs are becoming less attended; social clubs, societies and sports teams are closing down, and we observe notable shifts in people's confidence and independence as people realise that training in transferable skills, mobility and adaptability are more immediately important than needs of recognition and self-esteem. Withdrawal of social contact at the workplace can only have an adverse effect on teambuilding. The manager will no doubt have also recognised that some people take the short-cut to self-actualisation by leaving the organisation for the now not so mythical beach bar in Spain.

Lastly, let us now look at Herzberg's view of motivation as set out in his motivator–hygiene theory. Herzberg, in his work, demonstrates that man has two different sets of needs.

1. Lower-level needs that derive from man's desire to avoid pain and satisfy his basic needs (similar to Maslow).
2. Higher-level needs relating to that unique human characteristic, the ability to achieve and to experience psychological growth. (Included in these are the needs to achieve mastery over a difficult task and to earn – and receive – recognition.)

Team leaders have to look after the well-being of their team members as well as motivating them by satisfying their need for self-development.

Herzberg listed what he called hygiene factors (a common phrase of management) and said that if these are absent they would make employees feel exceptionally bad. They are extrinsic, i.e. they come from outside the individual. They also prevent dissatisfaction when they are adequate.

In ranked order of dissatisfaction these hygiene factors are as follows:

company policy and administration
supervision
relationship with supervisor
working conditions
salary
relationship with peers
personal life
relationship with team members
status
security

For the team leader, then, it is necessary to be aware of hygiene factors and their effects. We must accept that as management we can never get them totally right, but we must make sure that they are not causing dissatisfaction. The firm's canteen is a traditional but good example of a hygiene factor. If the canteen is perceived to be bad, then a great deal of dissatisfaction will be apparent throughout the organisation, even to the point of management receiving petitions; however, even if management spend a great deal of money on the canteen it will and can only be regarded as satisfactory. Most people will not notice its adequate functioning (they would notice it if it was not adequate!) and some people will always complain about the salads and the paintings on the walls.

Herzberg also listed motivator factors and how, if present in the job, these made employees feel exceptionally good. These factors are intrinsic, i.e. they come from inside the person. They lead to motivation when you build them into the way you manage your team.

In ranked order of ability to motivate people's preferences were:

achievement
recognition
work itself
responsibility

advancement
growth

The team leader should make sure that the members of the team are given the ability to achieve tasks, receive recognition for a job well done and provide opportunities for training, responsibility, promotion etc.

As part of motivation and teambuilding training we regularly use Herzberg's work, by a simple consensus exercise which is undertaken before a discussion of the motivator-hygiene theory.

Group exercise – employee goals

Team members are first asked to rank one to ten (ten being the highest award) what they as individuals want from their job. Then, in syndicate groups of between five and seven people, to agree by consensus what they as a group want, and then similarly what the staff want, and lastly what their management wants. The results are always consistent with Herzberg's findings and if there has been a psychological shift in the organisation due to management intervention, i.e. imposing a pay freeze, or making a round of redundancies, then those hygiene factors so disturbed will be ranked very highly. (See chart opposite.)

	Self	Group	Staff	Management
Feeling in on things				
Sympathetic help on personal problems				
Full appreciation of work done				
Tactful disciplining				
Personal loyalty to workers				
Interesting work				
Good working conditions				
Promotion and growth in company				
Job security				
Good wages				

12. MOTIVATING THE TEAM

'That typically English characteristic for which there is no
English name – *esprit de corps*.'

Frank Ezra Adcock

In order for teams to fulfil their full potential and achieve the set
tasks, there must be motivation. Having looked at motivation of
the individual we will now look at it in the team situation. If we
take a simple definition of motivation as being the willingness of
an individual to exert effort in order to achieve a goal or outcome
which will satisfy needs beyond personal needs, then team
motivation is simply the willingness of the team to do the same.
We know from experience of working with teams that it is better
for team leaders to have three people who work with them than
six who just labour for them. The question that then arises is if we
can motivate individuals, can we motivate the whole team in a
similar manner? Is motivation infectious; if – in a team of eight
people – five are well motivated, will this have a knock-on effect
for the other three?

Team leaders must also understand the difference between
morale and motivation. We will also consider in this chapter if the
team as a group can be offered inducements to perform which will
enhance the group rather than the individuals. The motivational
drives will often come down to the way the individual team member perceives the team's development on the one hand and on the
other hand the benefits to self.

As we saw before, if our early ancestor in the cave was
motivated to survival by necessity, then survival also required
that group behaviour replace individual behaviour and self-
motivation give way to team motivation. The most successful

hunter then became the leader, teacher and motivator of the group, which in turn became more proficient in hunting and the sense of group motivation became visible. The team was therefore offered group inducements in the form of killing more animals for food, and the individual's needs were satisfied by the most successful hunter–killer receiving the best cuts of meat. Individual needs for recognition and reward were also satisfied. The leader knowing then that through training and success the team was motivated could – like a coach – increase morale just before the hunt by recalling past glories which would give the group the keen edge and thereby increase the chance of a good hunt. Morale, then, is the final polish that is applied to a motivated team. We also know that in the early stages of teambuilding, there can be conflict between the aims of the person seeking to motivate others and the aims of the people being motivated. The skill and experience of the team leader then is in the ability to motivate the team without losing sight of the team members' individual goals, including the leader's own.

Team leaders, when appointed, often have had little or no training in how to motivate teams, and as in so much of our approach to management training it is something we pick up along the way. Often we take as a role model a manager we admire.

Team motivation will occur if three major things are present.

Communication

In Chapter 9 we looked at information flow and communication, and we saw that the team must know what it is doing and why. Discussion and debate is motivational, and will gain a higher degree of commitment than, say, giving orders. Communication is a vehicle to motivate, and we have seen that group discussions were often a precursor to agreement to a motivated action; for example the North American Indians' powwow.

Training

In Chapter 10 we considered training and how we can argue that a highly trained team is a motivated team. In other words, the individuals in the team must feel highly trained and competent to do the job. In the armed forces the senior officers quite rightly remind us that motivation and high morale are a function of, and a result of, years of intense and applied dedicated training. The Gulf War of 1991 showed very clearly the difference between highly trained and motivated armies, and depressed, untrained troops.

Resources

Communication and training, however, are not enough. The team must have the necessary resources of, in particular, money, people, equipment, authorisations and time in order to do the job. This chapter therefore concentrates on the problems of resourcing teams, and its effect upon motivation and morale. To use the armed forces again as an example, motivation and morale must include giving the teams the best equipment to undertake the task. Without the best equipment motivation will eventually disappear.

A team, whether a short-lived networking team or a long duration team, will only be motivated if the team members feel that there is a good chance that effort on behalf of the team will lead to obtaining some desired reward or goal. In Victor Vroom's expectancy model, a detailed analysis of which we will examine in Chapter 13, he points out that motivation will take place if two things occur.

1. If the value of the particular outcome is very high for the team.
2. If the team feels that they have a reasonably good chance of accomplishing the task and obtaining the outcome.

To put it more simply, if the prize offered is valued by the team and there is a good chance of winning it then motivation will arise.

The rewards for crime are presumably the same as they have ever been, but studies of crime have suggested that criminal activity is increasing precisely because various social and penal factors are conspiring to make the likelihood of obtaining the rewards more likely, making it more likely that they will 'get away with it'.

If, however, a barrier is placed in the way of the incentive or reward, then frustration will occur and motivation will not take place or will be lost. These barriers are often a lack of, or withdrawal of, resources necessary to do the job. In the case of crime, the barrier that is apparently not being put in the way is that of catching and successfully prosecuting criminals. Criminals are motivated by the lack of barriers; businesses should be so lucky.

The team leader's task is therefore to identify these barriers and then systematically start dismantling them.

Obviously some of the barriers are more apparent than real, and experience and challenge through open forum is needed to sort them into what we can call intangible and tangible.

Barriers to team motivation

We will now look at some examples of the intangible and tangible barriers that can lead to de-motivating teams, taken from our experience in many different types of organisations.

Intangible barriers which can be real or perceived

- Lack of senior management's commitment to the team or the task.
- Close adherence to out-of-date working practices in the belief that they are cemented in stone.
- Acting and behaving in such a way that may conform to the tradition of the organisation but quickly turns people off, failing to recognise their needs.
- Not being sure of our powers as individuals and leaving the team unaware of its collective authority and limitations.
- Using history and what has gone before as an excuse to find reasons why things cannot be done.
- Imagining existent or non-existent power blocks that may or may not frustrate the team's efforts.

Tangible barriers

- Social and environmental constraints.
- Out-of-date, worn out and poorly-maintained plant and equipment.
- Poor working conditions.

- Bad relationships with management, staff, workforce, suppliers and customers.
- Insufficient staff and lack of suitable training.
- Indecision by management.
- Time management constraints.
- Too low a level of authorisations for resources.

We have seen then that the team leader's job is not only to pull down such barriers but to establish their existence in the first instance with the team and then address the issues they raise with senior management.

Practical steps in team motivation

We will now turn to some practical steps in team motivation. The team leader must be aware of how to make members of the team feel valued, as well as providing scope for development, recognising achievements and providing challenge.

Feel valued

The team leader can make the team members feel valued by:

- holding short but regular meetings of the progress of the group;
- sharing and demonstrating an interest in whatever the team holds important;
- creating and nurturing an atmosphere of approval and co-operation;
- ensuring that each individual member of the team understands the importance of his or her contribution to the team's objectives;
- making sure that the team understands the purpose and goals of the organisation and why that particular part of the industry or commerce matters.

Provide scope for development

The team leader can facilitate team development by:

- providing on- and off-the-job training in skills and development;
- arranging and facilitating all necessary internal and external contacts, customers, suppliers etc.;
- using inter-team training and encouraging horizontal communications;
- agreeing sensible and achievable targets.

Recognise achievements

The team leader must recognise, and importantly make visible, achievements by:

- praising and communicating the team's success within the organisation and, where possible, to the outside world as well;
- reporting to senior management regularly on the team's progress and passing down to the team's senior management views and praise as well as criticism;
- holding regular tutorial sessions with individual members of the team to monitor and counsel on that individual's progress towards targets;
- communicating the company's and department's results and achievements, and how the team has contributed to such.

Provide challenge

The team leader must on behalf of the team provide challenge by:

- establishing and communicating the mutually agreed team's objectives;
- providing authorities and permissions enabling the team to take the greatest amount of responsibility possible;
- establishing a succession plan and the expectancy of promotion to team leader by thoroughly training up at least one deputy;
- fostering and encouraging ideas and challenges. Where practical the leader should allow the team to implement its ideas fully, even across corporate boundaries.

As we saw in Chapter 11 individuals have a set of past experiences which will affect their beliefs about the world around them, as well as other people and themselves. These in turn will affect the individual rights which a person attributes to themselves and allows to others. Again, these in turn will affect the person's behaviour towards others, both in what they say and what they do. Behaviour must be properly understood because the person's individual behaviour influences other people's behaviours. Most importantly – and this is perhaps not always fully appreciated – *a person's behaviour is the only part of us which is actually visible to others*.

In most circumstances we can choose the way in which we behave, and it is this awareness that we can then use to influence and motivate people around us. In order for the team leader to motivate the team it is vitally important that he or she be clear in his or her own mind what is of personal importance and to express those views with clarity and conviction. Professor Zander, in 1982, listed several points that are summarised below.

In order to influence people and thus motivate them you must do the following.

- You must know your own mind and recognise what beliefs are important to you, what goals you want to achieve and what direction you believe is appropriate for both you and your team.
- You must determine what effects inducements and coercions have upon you and your fellow team members.
- You must consider whether it is possible to respond to the requirements of team members without losing sight of your own individual goals or capitulating in a weak manner rather than responding in a positive one.
- You must decide whether you are prepared to give up personal preferences or reduce your own rights merely to prevent disharmony in your group.
- You must recognise when you have lost interest in a project or task, and find out what is necessary to re-energise that interest. Sometimes you must find an alternative person to take over the leadership of the group to finish the job.
- You must identify like-minded people and join forces with them.

- You must hold out against social pressures by concealing from others what you think, when disclosing your views would be to the detriment of the team effort.

The above notes can be regarded as guidelines to the position you are starting from when you are trying to influence motivational behaviour. It should be remembered that many persuasive styles such as the 'carrot' or the 'stick' will achieve short-term acceptance, but if persuasion is achieved through a more open and enlightened route, then often a deeper and more committed behaviour will ensue.

Carrot and stick methods of making people do things are not motivational and are part of the push style of influencing behaviour. Push styles amount to forcing people into doing something: they move people rather than motivate them. Normally it creates a win or lose situation and is best used to obtain a quick result where a more enlightened route just would not do. If your building is on fire you tell people to get out as quickly as possible, you do not hold a meeting and discuss with them what happened in the film *Towering Inferno* as the start of a programme of enlightenment designed to encourage them to feel motivated to leave.

Typical push styles include threats of authority, aggression, nagging, and pressurising and manipulation. As a result the recipient tends to lose face and will often seek revenge. Push styles are often demotivating over the longer term and would typically include rewards of a short-term nature, such as bribing people with additional money, promotion or free time. What tends to happen is that the reward quickly becomes a right and has to be constantly increased in order to obtain the same performance level from others. Some people can also feel insulted to be offered rewards, especially when the reward bears no comparison to the effort having been undertaken. Money can only be used as a recognition of achievement, not as a bribe towards achievement.

Influencing through a pull style, i.e. pulling people towards us, is motivational. Pull styles create a situation where the person wants to perform certain tasks; however pull styles must be used sincerely and not in a manipulative or dishonest manner. Used correctly, pull styles lead to a more committed and increased effort, and they are morale building. Pull styles create vision and lead to higher quality performance and challenge in the organisation. This style is possibly slower to achieve results because of the element of longer-term commitment through meaningful debate, challenge and thought, but once in place it is more difficult to dislodge the results. Pull styles demand certain ways of behaving and require personal disclosure on the part of the team leader who will seek from the team co-operation by saying things like 'I have a problem, and I need your help'. This invariably means that there must be openness and the team leader must display honesty and truthfulness, indeed he or she must have a reputation for this or there will be distrust.

Pull styles allow responsibility, project ownership and commitment on the part of others. They must include giving recognition and praise, they require active rather than passive listening and will work most effectively if the team leader is seen to be excited by the commitment of others, enthusiastically sharing the hopes and visions of the team. It must be remembered that you cannot use a push style and then hope to apply a pull style. The unenlightened attitudes, the win–lose situation and the lack of committed action caused by push styles mean that you cannot then hope to 'gloss over' the damage caused. Time permitting, the team leader should apply a pull style and if the pull style is not working then – at least with regard to short-term crisis management – push styles can be used to achieve certain short-term goals.

Lastly, we have devised a motivational checklist in the hope that the team leader will apply some of the ideas in his or her teambuilding activities.

1. People behave in anticipation of positive reward. Such rewards should therefore always be based on performance and given as soon as possible after the desired performance. Remember what motivates one person may not necessarily motivate another.

2. Eliminate unnecessary threats and punishments; they only lead to and encourage avoidance behaviour, especially team avoidance.

3. Make sure that accomplishment is adequately recognised.

All people need to feel important, no matter how modest their position in the organisation.

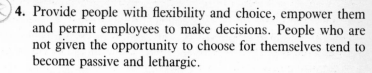

4. Provide people with flexibility and choice, empower them and permit employees to make decisions. People who are not given the opportunity to choose for themselves tend to become passive and lethargic.

5. Provide support when it is needed. Employees should be encouraged to ask for support and assistance. Asking for help should not be considered a sign of weakness.

6. Provide teams with responsibility along with accountability. Few people will reject accountability as long as the tasks in question are within their areas of responsibility, and the skill base of the individual or the team. Equally, they will enjoy responsibility if they can see that the results will reflect on them or their team.

7. Encourage employees and teams to set their own goals or at least to participate actively in the goal-setting process. There will be failures; see them, and ensure that others see them, as part of the learning process. To 'punish' failure even by intolerant body language is to encourage people not to take risks; and risks are essential to creativity.

8. Make sure that employees are aware of how their tasks relate to the organisational goals. Routine work can result in passivity and boredom unless employees and teams are aware of how these tasks contribute to the goals of the total organisation.

9. Make sure that your team members fully understand your expectations.

10. Permit your team to experience the personal satisfaction of doing an appropriately challenging job well.

11. Consider your verbal behaviour. Use people's individual names, encourage your team members to have their say and express their views. Interact with them and check that you and the others have understood their contribution. Acknowledge the team's views and ideas by paraphrasing what has been said.

12. Consider your non-verbal behaviour. Sit with your team members, not behind your desk. Adopt an open and relaxed posture and smile. Look directly at them when speaking and maintain good eye contact at all times. Use facial expressions to emphasise certain points and do not be afraid to gesture, taking care of course to avoid offensive gestures. Where appropriate, inject humour into the situation.

13. Accept and design projects and tasks on behalf of your team to be consistent with the team's needs of affiliation, approval and achievement.

14. Even in team situations treat all employees as individuals.

15. Provide your team with immediate and relevant feedback; never give negative evaluative feedback without providing information why.

16. Recognise and – with your team – eliminate barriers to individual and team achievement.

17. Exhibit confidence in your team. Teams who are expected to achieve will do so more frequently than those who are expected to fail.

18. Increase the likelihood that teams will experience accomplishment. It's an old cliché, but it is true that nothing succeeds like success.

19. Exhibit interest in, and knowledge of, each individual team member.

20. Encourage teams to participate in making decisions that affect them. Individuals and teams who have no control over their destiny become passive, viewing the control of their lives as external to themselves. This can result in learned helplessness.

21. Establish a climate of trust and open communication. Motivation is highest in teams that are empowered.

22. Teams must be able to recognise that their tasks are related to the output of the organisation or the department.

23. Listen to and deal effectively with team members' fears and

complaints. Team problems can greatly reduce effectiveness when they are not dealt with.

24. Frequently point out improvement in performance during the early stages of teambuilding.

25. The team leader is a motivator, and therefore must be motivated. Modelling appropriate behaviour and attitude is a powerful tool.

26. Criticise behaviour, not people. A person can do a task poorly and still be a valuable member of the team. Negative feedback of team members on performance should never focus on the performer as an individual, e.g. 'dumb', 'stupid', 'lazy' etc.

27. Make sure that team effort pays off in results. If effort does not pay off there will be a tendency to stop trying.

28. Anxiety is fundamental to team motivation. The total elimination of task-anxiety can result in lethargy; however, very high anxiety can result in disorientation and ineffectiveness.

29. Be concerned with short-term and long-term motivation. Teams who receive only short-term reinforcement and incentives tend to fall short of optimal motivation. They will tend to lack a long-term perspective on team work.

30. Avoid motivation overkill.

13. MOTIVATION AND MORALE

> 'Appetite comes with eating.'
>
> François Rabelais

Managers and team leaders are continuing to express concern about effective strategies for motivating employees. Those models of motivation which take into account how individuals deal with information normally make the following two assumptions.

1. The individual learns to expect that specific types of behaviour will produce clear positive or negative outcomes.
2. The individual is capable of working out the perceived value of the consequences of the above.

The team leader must remember, when seeking to motivate the team, that there is a direct relationship between the actions and behaviour of an individual and the value that the individual puts on the perceived outcome.

Three important questions should be answered prior to the team leader commencing to try to motivate others.

1. What type of expectations does the individual have concerning the work environment?
2. What type of linkages does the individual employee perceive exists between different types of behaviours at work and the outcomes of those behaviours?
3. What does the individual value?

What people expect from their efforts at any given time can be influenced by the team leaders; they can indicate most clearly the link between behaviour and the consequences of that behaviour. However, influencing people's values is not

166

easy and it can be argued that the discovery and provision of what individuals value in the work environment is an area that has yet to be fully explored by managers in UK organisations.

Up to the present there has been a total preoccupation with individual rewards over which most managers and team leaders have little or no control, such as salaries and bonuses. In addition we have often been persuaded that money is what employees value most. Managers and team leaders who agree with this idea, but have little or no control over employees' remuneration, sometimes wrongly come to the conclusion that the organisation stops them from being able effectively to motivate their team members.

A more complete understanding of the problems associated with an over-reliance upon money as the primary motivator of team members can be gained by dividing rewards and punishment into two categories: intrinsic (those things that come from within us) and extrinsic (those things that come from outside).

We can define intrinsic rewards as those outcomes of work behaviour that an individual values, but which are not recognised formally within the organisation. For example, the performance of a specific task by an individual may provide the person with substantial mental stimulation, even though the job completion does not normally lead to more tangible rewards, such as increased salary.

Extrinsic rewards generally include more tangible assets which are provided through more formal business lines and include salary as well as promotion, company cars etc. Organisations competing for the same types of skills within a specific labour market normally conduct surveys of these extrinsic rewards to ensure that they are competitive with all those other organisations recruiting in the same labour market. Consequently, the existence of relatively equal extrinsic rewards between similar organisations increases the importance of the perceived intrinsic rewards. This means that if two companies are offering the same remuneration package then an individual will select the company to join based on the perceived intrinsic rewards likely. Both authors have worked in organisations where the perception of the intrinsic rewards was fundamental in attracting young graduates and professional staff; these were named as training, career progression and the likelihood of foreign travel.

Team leaders must, therefore, recognise the strengths and validity of the intrinsic rewards being offered in their organisation so that these can be communicated.

It would be wrong to assume that individuals in a given work environment are always trying to observe and assess the consequences of their behaviour, and seeking reward. Empirical observation and case studies exist which clearly demonstrate that when an individual has been able to identify a certain pattern of behaviour which then produces desired outcomes, the probability of these individuals continuing to assess alternative behaviour is greatly reduced. Looking at it from another viewpoint, the newly-learned behaviours begin to become somewhat habitual. When behaviours become habitual, they are more difficult to influence. For the team leader, then, effectively to influence these behaviours, he must stimulate individuals to reconsider the consequences of the habits they have now fallen into. This is a very difficult task. The more ingrained the habit in an individual (and the organisation), the harder the task of changing it. An example that we are continually coming up against in industry and commerce is the ingrained working patterns of middle management who cannot see any weakness in those habits that actually promoted them; they therefore become resistant to change.

The only way we can change these habits is by refocusing the attention of the individual upon both intrinsic and extrinsic rewards associated with the behaviours which have now become habitual. In essence, it requires raising an individual's level of self-awareness. The individual must be stimulated to take a very close inward look at him or herself to examine his or her own current needs and how these needs are being satisfied or not being satisfied through the behavioural patterns which are being pursued. Obviously, it is often the case that those behavioural patterns now being exhibited do not produce outcomes which satisfy the individual's needs. The example below will help clarify this point.

Often in many organisations morale is low. When this happens, managers, team leaders and supervisors articulate the promise that if employee morale could be increased, then an increase in productivity would follow. Unfortunately, managers and team leaders treat the morale problem as an event or an organisational state totally independent of themselves. That is, they do not perceive that they are capable of having any impact upon the morale problem. Interestingly enough, in these types of situations, managers may themselves contribute substantially to the existence of the morale problem. If managers project a negative attitude concerning the state of affairs in a given organisation, it is quite predictable that team members will exhibit a similar negative attitude. Consequently, the success of any intervention policy designed to increase employee morale is contingent upon managers changing their attitudes and becoming positive – and not negative – role models. The only way that managers and team leaders can increase morale is by challenging their own attitudes and changing them so that they project positive behaviour which will be interpreted by the individuals as support and commitment.

Morale problems are intimately associated with motivation, productivity, customer service and quality. These variables are also related to both the intrinsic and extrinsic rewards that can be secured by an individual in the organisation. Understanding and appreciating the interrelationships among these variables can be better explained by using a model that briefly demonstrates these relationships at work. The model below gives guidelines to identify possible courses of action that management can take to improve individual motivation, thereby adding value to the organisation.

Vroom's motivation model is based on a school of thought that individuals will follow a path leading to a goal if they expect it to lead to some reward or satisfaction of need.

We can define expectancy as the belief that an individual has that he will achieve the task and be rewarded for doing so.

Outcome rewards can include factors such as job security, promotion, money and good working conditions. Outcome needs encompass those areas that can be satisfied through obtaining the outcome rewards, such as food, shelter, status and work satisfaction.

Therefore, we can argue that if employees see high productivity or quality work as a path leading to the attainment of one or more of their personal goals, then they will tend to be high producers,

Vroom's (1964) model of motivation:

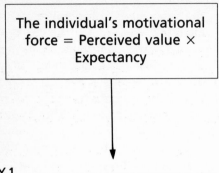

The individual's motivational force = Perceived value × Expectancy

EXPECTANCY 1 ....

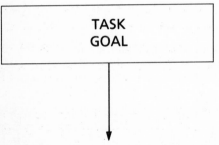

TASK
GOAL

EXPECTANCY 2 ....

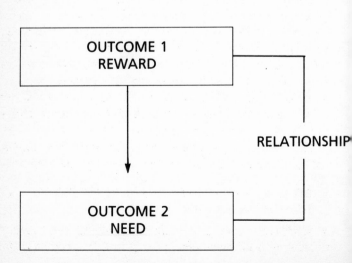

OUTCOME 1
REWARD

RELATIONSHIP

OUTCOME 2
NEED

or quality employees; conversely if they see low productivity as a path to the achievement of those goals, they will tend to be low producers.

We can then see that if a factory or office is in danger of closure after it has completed its allotted task, and the individual wishes to retain his or her job, we must not be surprised if low effort and low productivity ensues, if that person perceives this to be the path to the goal of job security (i.e. holding back to make the job last longer). Should we be surprised that shipbuilders are not particularly in a hurry to finish the last ship on the stocks before the yard is closed?

Individual productivity, then, is all about a person's own motivation to do something at a given level of performance. In turn the motivation depends upon:

- the particular needs of the individual likely to be satisfied by the goals towards which he or she is moving;

- the individual's perception regarding the relevance of working behaviour in the relationship between outcome needs and outcome rewards.

The model clearly indicates a relationship between outcome rewards and outcome needs. For example, if the individual does not think he or she can accomplish the task that has been assigned, it logically follows that attainment of outcome rewards (and satisfaction of outcome needs) becomes academic and motivation to perform will be low. Assuming the individual can accomplish the task, but does not perceive that the outcome reward associated with it will be forthcoming, then the individual is not going to be highly motivated to complete the task. If the outcome rewards are not perceived as being instrumental in satisfying outcome needs, it is unlikely that an individual is going to be highly motivated to perform.

The team leader, when looking at the motivation of the individual members of the team, can ask some pertinent questions.

- Are team members being assigned tasks they are capable of doing? If not, why not?

- What types of rewards, both extrinsic and intrinsic, are being given to team members for successful task completions?

171

- What types of intrinsic rewards that could be provided to team members for successful task completion are being ignored?

- What are the relationships that exist between the rewards being provided to team members and their own personal needs?

The team leader will readily see that to the extent that these questions are not addressed and corrective action taken where needed, it is unlikely that a motivated team will be developed within the organisation.

A good example of effective motivation and high morale can be seen in the Apple Mackintosh story. The founder and chairman of Apple Mackintosh, in order to compete with IBM, decided with his colleagues that he would lead the development team for the new user-friendly product. He recruited and built, using young staff, a team that were divorced from the rules and regulations of the organisation. They had their own building (from which they flew the 'Jolly Roger'!), they could dress as they pleased, come and go as they pleased and were consulted at every level of the development. The rewards and recognition offered hand-in-hand with the risk were extremely high. Motivation and morale were very high. In a short space of time they developed the Apple Mac, probably the most advanced personal computer of its time.

Less dramatic examples include the 'competitiveness' of different shift teams in, for example, mining and oil platforms (who can dig the most coal, lay the most pipe, etc.).

14. *NGAHAU TOA*

Teambuilding principles, as this book shows, have changed dramatically over the years. The new approaches towards the team providing for the needs and desires of its individual members is relatively new; the earliest team principles were concerned only that the team should function with unity for the Corporate Good.

Techniques of teambuilding have changed; for example, we have been involved in pioneering work in bringing the energies of the performing arts to the business world – with great success.

The future will hold still more changes, no doubt, but for large companies teambuilding is probably as radical as can be accepted at the present time. Even when every member of a large multinational organisation agrees on a new path to follow, pushing the corporation down that path can take many years; the force needed to move mountains is always immense, even with the right fulcrum. However, in small businesses teambuilding is just as vital, though it is often overlooked in books on the subject. And being small, strikingly radical changes can be made relatively swiftly. The results can be revealing; and perhaps show a glimpse of the future.

We have been closely associated with two small organisations that have undergone very radical teambuilding, indeed their whole corporate design is innovative. We are grateful to these organisations for sharing their experiences with us. Much of the work in these organisations was done by a consultant with whom we have worked, Tracey Bronlund, a New Zealander whose Maori motto – displayed on her business cards – gives this chapter its title. *Ngahau toa* means, literally, 'Encouragement and support for the brave warrior'. In this case the brave warrior in question is anyone in the organisation prepared to risk themselves in enterprise; the organisation is required to give as much support to that idea as possible.

It is an idealised principle which takes empowerment and personal development further than usual. The basic principle is that every member of the team has an equally valuable contribution to make and that innovative thinking is not the domain of particular individuals. It recognises that the MD or the tea-boy are equally likely to see opportunities and that they should be encouraged to share them. Indeed, if it is the tea-boy that comes up with an innovative idea he would be appointed team leader, the MD may be one of the support-team – perhaps helping him through the complexities of corporate life with which he might be unfamiliar. It has effective results; the MD may not hear internal complaints about the company, but the tea-boy might well do so. Certainly, the receptionist will hear many comments from outside about the company; these may be valuable.

The ideal team treats every member of the company as its eyes and ears, its arms and legs. If the tea-boy has no power to contribute then the company is to that degree blind, to that degree crippled.

Another innovation is that every member of the company is given the opportunity to be what they want to be. In one of the companies one of the typists discovered that she wanted to be involved with customers. The environment was set up to allow her to spend time working with customers. In fact she discovered that she wanted direct face-to-face involvement which this company simply could not provide and she left to work in retail. However, she would not have discovered her own needs but for the company, and the company shed a worker who would not have been fulfilled by working for it; just as its principles would attract many to it who would be fulfilled, who would make valuable contributions, but who traditional job placements would have overlooked.

Probably the most innovative principle was that its customers were valuable members of the company's team. In a literal way. Large companies have recognised customer focus for its value, but have dealt with it by working more closely with the customers. In these smaller companies product development was undertaken with the customers' own consultants who were part of the team. They literally shared in the decision-making processes. Of course, such a system only works where there is sufficient trust; indeed it only works where the other companies have similar principles. Such companies are few, and generally small, but the future may hold an expansion of this.

To facilitate the above, a company requires a 'project control' which is regarded as the heart of the corporate body. It is designed to ensure that all teams are provided with the necessary environment in which to function. This can mean either the physical environment or the attitude of team members; project control is 'Mother' to every employee – it deals with their needs so that they can deal with their work. When a team is 'blocked' because – perhaps – it lacks certain skills, then project control will locate those skills, often from unlikely places.

One of the companies we are discussing now 'failed'; it collapsed into liquidation. Ironically, however, at least part of that failure was due to the imposition of 'traditional' business methods over the innovative principles.

The company had been totally 'open'. Access to the MD, the working owners and anyone else was available to all. It was better than an 'open door' policy – there were simply no doors at all. The individual who created the company did so from his vision of what he believed he could do. He shared that vision with his whole team, and they regularly discussed it with no hierarchical barriers. The empowerment was astonishing; not one member of that company would have failed to put in the necessary overtime willingly to meet a deadline, or would not have made significant changes to their lifestyles in order to move the vision forward. They genuinely saw it as their vision as much as that of the owner.

Unfortunately, financial support from a foreign company was withdrawn – due to that company's own problems in fact – which caused a crisis in this company. Even then the MD of the company told us, 'This is an opportunity for us'; there was no sense of failure. But the financial problems had to be addressed and a 'traditional' manager was brought in to deal with the crisis. He was not empowered by the vision; indeed his greatest concern seemed to be what class of company car he would have. Worse, he shared the vision with the owner, but regarded it as something to be 'handed down' to the company, not shared with 'the lower orders'. Access to the owner was cut off, except through this new

175

manager. Dissatisfaction set in, there was no longer room for personal development; virtually just, 'Do as you're told'. The most innovative members of the company left; those that remained were those who were happy to do what they were told, not those who wanted to create. The company died of apathy.

Perhaps a happy ending lies at the end of their rainbow, however. Even total collapse was viewed as an opportunity by the owner. He recreated his old company and found new backers, though on a slightly smaller scale. The manager was not re-employed, but many of the former creative members were. The signs are that the new company is heading for success for itself and all its individuals. Certainly, it may lay down part of a model for the future.

15. TEAM MEETINGS

'Committee – a group of men who keep minutes and waste hours.'

Milton Berle

There will be times when the team must come together in formal meetings. This is not to suggest that informal gatherings are to be avoided, indeed they can be essential for team cohesiveness and motivation, but this chapter is concerned with a particular type of gathering, the formal meeting. The frequency of such meetings will depend on the team's purpose; they may be regular, or *ad hoc*, or a combination of both, and they will take place at intervals of time to suit the tasks in hand.

Team meetings are crucial to teambuilding and morale; they are the place for effective decision-making, for airing both positive and negative views, and they are a forum for debate. People in teams need 'their say' and feel involved if they not only get it, but know that channels of communication exist to relate their feelings and opinions throughout the organisation. The team meeting, run well, can be that necessary forum. Badly run, they can undo a great deal of teambuilding effort in the workplace.

We must first consider what a meeting is and when it is the essential form of gathering. To do this most effectively we can look at when meetings are *not* necessary.

Some meetings are held to disseminate information and do not require any feedback from the information-receivers. It may be that some form of personal presentation is thought to be necessary and in exceptional circumstances a meeting may be the best way to provide the information. However, it must be remembered that even the arranging of meetings takes time and in most organisations there is premium time on meeting rooms requiring that their use be limited only to the essential.

Memos

A more cost-effective form of disseminating information might simply be the issue of a memo. Even if the memo runs to several pages it can then be read by the individuals at times convenient to themselves without any disruption of working time. It would then be possible, if required, to arrange a short meeting to bring the team together simply for feedback on the points raised by the memo, and even then those points should be notified to the chair before the meeting is called so that attendees of the meeting will have some idea of what the topics for discussion are going to be. If reading effectively the memo would take one hour and the feedback time perhaps a quarter of an hour; then a great many workhours would be saved by avoiding the necessity of having the whole team silently gathered around a conference table reading independently.

There are drawbacks to the use of memos, the most obvious of which is that they can be downgraded in importance and are often not read at all. These drawbacks can be overcome in two ways. First, to be effective a memo should be 'user-friendly', in other words it must be drafted in a way that makes reading easy. Effective report writing is an essential basic skill that is worth the trouble to learn well. Secondly, any important points raised in the memo should always be followed up, so that those not reading the memos will be continually 'caught out' and will learn to read them next time!

There is a third back-up in modern organisations which is the use of electronic mail ('E' mail). 'E' mail provides for the issue of memos through linked computer circuits and has the added advantage of displaying a note to the sender that the memo has been read by the receiver. Those who simply clear their memos off the screen without reading them will soon be identified as such. With 'E' mail there can be no claiming that the memo didn't reach them, somehow fell down the back of a cabinet, got lost in the in-tray etc.

Telephone meetings

In many cases meetings of whole teams, perhaps twelve people or so, are called and the end result is ten people watching two other people talk. If a matter can be settled between two people without the need of others, if their input is not useful, then a meeting should be avoided and those two people should contact each other either by telephone or simply walking down the corridor and peering around the other's office door. Again, there are obviously disadvantages. Meetings allow for preparation whereas surprise encounters do not. Even then, if preparation time is needed then a simple phone call suggesting that 'Could you have such and such ready for a given time and I will call you back then. . .' is better than wasting a lot of other people's time. Face-to-face meetings and phone calls also suffer from the master/servant mentality; in other words there is usually somebody demanding information or giving instructions and somebody receiving the demand or the instruction. There is no true interaction, no chair to mediate between parties and no third party to suggest other courses or options. None the less, for many situations where meetings are wrongfully called, these forms of communication are quite adequate and far more cost-effective.

Multi-gang communications

Taking telephone calls one stage further, most modern organisations now have telephone systems enabling multi-gang communications, in other words several people on the same telephone call. This is clearly closer to a meeting and does allow for input beyond two people. It somewhat reduces the master/servant mentality, but it still suffers from a great many limitations. As we shall see when we look at the organisation of 'proper meetings', the chair must be very active in keeping the meeting energised. Even where a multi-gang telephone link does have a Chair it is very difficult for that person to ensure the full participation of all parties when they cannot be seen.

Furthermore, verbal communication accounts for only 20 per cent of total communication; telephone calls sacrifice the other 80 per cent. One manager constantly in telephone 'breakfast' meetings told us that he had no sympathy for such meetings and would put his phone down, eat his breakfast, and occasionally pick up the phone and make a small contribution to show he was still there. Heaven knows how effective the meetings were if all the delegates did the same thing, but certainly the manager we spoke to indicated that he had never been 'caught out'!

Video link meetings

Taking telephone calls to a third stage, there is the possibility of video link meetings where there is some ability for participants to see each other. An account manager for a major telecommunications company says that there was a massive surge in demand for video link facilities when company directors who might be spread across several continents felt unwilling to fly to meetings because of the Gulf crisis.

One or two directors have already been heard to say that if such communications were successful, then 'All those expensive flights to Rio, Hong Kong etc. can obviously be taken out of next year's budgets as they won't be needed then either'. There will no doubt be a great deal of back-tracking and people arguing how ineffective non face-to-face communication is in the future! Sarcasm aside, there are times when nothing can replace face-to-face meetings and this should be borne in mind, though undoubtedly there have probably been a great many Atlantic crossings by Concorde when British Telecom could have done the flight more cost-effectively.

This question of face-to-face meetings is a vital one. One major organisation had whole office suites full of staff working at independent workstations, each self-contained in their own little world. Then the company decided that there were a great many costs to be saved from paying rent, leases etc., by sending all of the staff back to their homes supplied with their workstations. They would be reimbursed for any inconveniences, allowing the company to better use, or dispense with, its offices. The result was a collapse of that part of that organisation. It seemed, on hindsight analysis, that a vital part of keeping the organisation together was the time spent chatting at the coffee machine, up and down corridors, standing next to each other in the toilets and wherever else. It emphasised the point which is made throughout this book and which we have made many times in our very extensive work in teambuilding; i.e. that teambuilding is not logical, it's psychological.

Meetings with a purpose

From the above, we can begin to see exactly what the formal meeting actually is. It is a time when the whole team, or selected members of the team, possibly with invited outside expertise or input, come together for a purpose.

'For a purpose' means exactly what it says. The purpose of the meeting should be defined well before the meeting is called and everybody called to the meeting should be aware of what the purpose is. Meetings may be designed to solve problems, to update the team on individual or sub-team progress, to produce recommendations to be put forward to others, or any number of other purposes. It is important that all members of the team are aware of precisely what is required of them so that they may adequately prepare for the meeting. Planned time is worth much more than unplanned time, and the meeting will be more cost-effective, more expedient and more rewarding for participants if everyone involved understands the direction that the meeting is intended to move in.

Meetings serve two overall functions. First, they are a vital part of communication. They are obviously a form of communication between team members, but they also serve as a channel for information flow into the team and from the team to the outside world. Properly planned and properly organised they are a very cost-effective form of communication. Equally, badly planned and badly organised meetings are an enormous waste of effort and time on everybody's part, and indeed can often be a barrier to effective communication.

Secondly, meetings form a vital part of the corporate learning process. Clearly there is a direct learning function in that team members learn of the work or progress of other team members, but more subtle learning is also going on. Subordinates are learning about their bosses, and bosses are learning about their subordinates; their strengths and weaknesses, where they can and cannot be relied on, and those who are and who are not well organised. As such it should not be understated that good performance in meetings is part of a significant career development. As an obvious example, if your boss asks you to attend a meeting in his or her stead and you prepare well, perform well at the meeting and represent him or her effectively, this is one of the building blocks of trust and reliance which lead to promotion. Failing to prepare well, performing badly at the meeting and representing your boss in a poor light will obviously result in your not being entrusted with important tasks in the future and, if this reflects your work attitude generally, could ultimately result in your boss asking that euphemistic question: 'Tell me, how long have you worked for the company? Not counting today, of course.'

Planning your meetings

In order that effective use of time is to be made, the arrangements for the meeting must be thoroughly planned.

The room

We can first look at the environment itself. The room size must be adequate for the purpose of the team. It is a ludicrous fact of corporate life that quite often teams end up adapting to suit the room available, rather than the desirable opposite of this. A team which should properly require, say, ten people ends up with only six, because there is nowhere to house a meeting of ten. It would be impossible to overstate the stupidity of such a position and clearly 'the tail must never wag the dog'. If a team of ten is required, then a room adequate for the requirements of a meeting of ten is equally necessary.

As to size itself, the room should never be claustrophobic and there should be far more room than merely sufficient seating space. Obviously, there must be room for adequate tables and chairs, but the room might also need to accommodate presentations and therefore may require white boards, flip charts, overhead projector screens etc. It might also be useful if the room could have 'a recreation spot'; somewhere where the team can mill around, drink coffee, talk informally outside the meeting time and so on. This begins to establish the room as a centre point for the team in more than just meetings. It is important to remember that air, space and openness encourage freer thinking, higher levels of energy and a wider focus of purpose. Tight, closed, cramped rooms lead to tight, closed, cramped thinking.

The organisation of the furnishings will depend partly on the purpose of the meeting. As a general rule long, rectangular tables are particularly suited to hierarchical groups where, traditionally, the Chair is seated at the head of the table and the 'pecking order' of the team members can be determined by their proximity to that position. As an alternative, round tables deliberately discount both status and seniority, and allow for easier communications, particularly in problem-solving type meetings which require the breakdown of status barriers to facilitate free input.

The agenda

The direction and purpose of the meeting are dictated by the agenda, which is probably one of the most underrated documents ever devised. It is our experience that very few agendas are properly drafted, and that most are barely even adequate for the purpose. A typical agenda may well include only a date, time and place, a list of those to be present and a number of three or four word headings indicating the topics to be discussed. In fact, such an agenda is about as much good as a chocolate teapot, but for most companies a chocolate teapot is all they ever had to make the tea with and so they 'make do'. We have introduced the china teapot of agendas into several companies, all of whom have been astonished and delighted at the hundreds of work-hours saved as a result of adequate planning.

The usual stated aims of the agenda are threefold. The first is to confirm the place, date and times of the forthcoming meeting. Even though the minutes of any previous meeting will also contain this information, there may have been changes and in any case you should never pass up the opportunity to better ensure success.

The second aim of the agenda is to give members prior warning of what will be discussed at the meeting. This is of paramount importance, since members will be able to prepare their own input to the meeting in advance which will greatly speed up the meeting, make contributions more relevant, keep people to the timetable and generally focus the meeting more directly on the points to be dealt with.

The third aim of the Agenda is to guide members through the meeting indicating not only what is to be discussed, but the order in which items will be discussed. This is particularly useful for planning the timetable of the agenda, but we shall look at this later.

There is, however, a fourth aim of the agenda which, although it is often alluded to, is rarely used to its main benefit. This could best be summed up as 'to present a manageable list of items which can be adequately discussed in the time available'. This would seem to be the recipe for a timetable and indeed timetable it is. But this is not all that it is. Consider rephrasing the above as 'to produce a manageable number of items which can be adequately produced in the time available'. Yes, what we are actually looking at is more than a timetable, it is actually a production target and there is no reason why the agenda cannot act as a production target.

To be effective targets have two main criteria. The first of these is that they should be difficult to achieve. If they are easy to achieve, then people will not stretch themselves to achieve them or they will achieve them and then sit back and rest on their laurels. Translating that into meetings, if the agenda allows five hours for discussion of something that could be discussed in half an hour, then the meeting will take five hours and the most astute members of the team will consider it time well wasted. On the other hand a production target should be attainable with effort. If it is unattainable then no effort will be made even to set out on the task.

For example, if the agenda lists sixty items to be discussed, when in fact twenty items is the most that could possibly be covered, then those who should be preparing for items twenty-one to sixty will not even bother and furthermore they will know that their attendance at the meeting is going to be of limited value – if any at all – and this will have a demoralising effect on them and the meeting generally. An effective target is therefore attainable, but not easily attainable. If twenty items is a reasonable number and there is a surplus of items to be discussed then list twenty-five. If all goes well the backlog of items that have been carried forward in the past will be eaten away until the agenda is down to a manageable list of proper items to be discussed. On the other hand, once that has been achieved, or if in fact there is no surplus of items to be discussed, then consider the time usually given for the agenda which might be, say, three hours and make it two-and-a-half hours and focus everybody's attention on cutting down the meeting time.

Either way, by using the agenda as a production target, meetings will become more concise, more focused, people will feel better at the expediency of meetings and will gain by having more planned time available for other work.

The china teapot of agendas then, to which we referred earlier, should, of course, have a heading which specifies the title of the meeting, where it is to be held and the date on which it is to be held.

The heading should also contain the starting time and the proposed finishing time of the meeting. This latter point is very rarely listed, yet it is vital for good time planning. If our meeting is proposed to start at, say, 10 a.m. and there is no indication of a proposed finishing time, then those attending the meeting which may be, say, twelve people, all have to leave the rest of the day clear. In fact they may all be out of the meeting by 12 o'clock which will then leave them the majority of the day to work. However, none of the team members, subordinates or bosses will know that they are available, no appointments will have been made for them and the time available for work will be unplanned time rather than planned time, which is never so effective. By giving a proposed finishing time, then, after a reasonable (and reasonably short!) allowance for overruns they can make plans for the rest of the day. Twelve people with, say, five hours of time, represents some sixty hours of planned time as opposed to unplanned time – a massive increase in effective time. There is also a 'knock-on' effect; people who are able to arrange meetings with the individual team members are themselves able to plan their own days better. There is a further important advantage from having a proposed start and finish time which is examined below, when we look at the progress of the meeting itself.

There is also something very important about the list of people to be present. Many companies merely list all the people who are proposed to be at the meeting and, generally speaking, all of those people will arrive at the beginning and leave at the end. We have literally lost count of the amount of people questioned either during on-site operations or training courses who have complained of meetings, 'I spend at least half the time gazing at the ceiling wondering why I am there. . .'. And usually they are perfectly correct. All meetings include certain people who have to be there throughout, the Chair and the Secretary are the most obvious examples, but many people simply do not need to be present throughout the whole meeting. Either their input is restricted to one or two agenda items, or they are there simply to receive information from one or two particular areas of the meeting's agenda. In both cases they can be invited to attend for a limited period of time, freeing them for planned work outside the meeting time.

In other words, if, during a five-hour meeting, three of the people there need only be there for one hour instead of five, then twelve work-hours are immediately released by the simple expedience of planning the meeting in order to allow them to be available for just a brief period of time. Meetings do not run like clockwork and therefore some flexibility needs to be given but, as we shall see, meetings can be made to run more like clockwork than the headless chickens they often are.

Having established start and finish times and times for certain people to be invited, then clearly we are able to appoint proposed times to each agenda item. Our agenda is therefore now timetabled and will allow for effective planning by all members in a number of ways. For one thing, execution concentrates the mind wonderfully; if an item is targeted for a compact period of meeting time, then there is less likelihood of people rambling on and on as they will seek to 'make the target'. There is also an added advantage for team members, particularly inexperienced or nervous ones. As the meeting progresses along its agenda they will have forewarning of when their own major area is coming up, particularly an area where they may be making some sort of presentation. This will enable them to 'psyche themselves up', ready to do their bit.

The framework of the agenda
Now we come to the question of the framework of the agenda itself.

The first item on the agenda is usually '*Apologies for absence*'. At this point the Chair or Secretary will announce those people who were to be present who are no longer going to be there. There will always be occasions when, at the last minute, people ring in to say that they have been taken ill, delayed in transit and so on. If this is notified to the Secretary well ahead of time, then the Secretary has a responsibility to ensure that the absence of particular people does not mean that the meeting should be postponed, or more probably that certain sections of the meeting should be post-poned. If this is the case then it may be that one or two of the people who are being summoned to the meeting can be told not to turn up for the newly foreshortened meeting and they can be released for planned other useful time.

Obviously, there will be some cases of apologies for absence which take place on the very morning of the meeting in which case a certain amount of planned time will be lost, but it can be minimised if the Secretary, prior to or at the very beginning of the meeting, depending on when he or she is notified, immediately does the same check and if necessary announces to two or three people there that they will not be needed. Although they will then be released on unplanned time, rather than planned time, it will be more productive than finding out three hours into the meeting that in fact they are not needed. All team members should know that, unless otherwise notified, it is the Secretary to whom apolo-gies for absence should be given as he or she will be the central co-ordinator of the organisation of the meeting.

The second item relates to *Minutes of the last meeting*. Obviously, this applies where we are dealing with regular or sequential meetings, but the object of this heading is to review the minutes of the previous meeting and to approve them as a true record of that meeting. This is not the point at which twelve people should put their heads down and read the previous minutes for an hour or so; first, it is a total waste of time, particu-larly if some of the people had already correctly read through the minutes prior to the meeting and are now sitting around tapping their fingers.

On receiving the minutes of the meeting, which should be distributed as soon as possible after the meeting and therefore considerably before the next, all the team members should immediately read through the minutes to ensure that they are correct. Therefore, at this point on the agenda, only five minutes or so need be allocated to take the points which team members raise and if necessary correct the proper entry in the records. This is essential because some meetings may be a month or more apart and people will have forgotten what actually did happen at the meeting, particularly if there has been out-of-meeting discussion about matters in the interim. Ideally, the minutes should be distributed within forty-eight hours of the meeting and read within twenty-four hours of that. This also means that the previous meeting will not be entirely debated again at this point on this agenda.

The third item is usually '*Matters arising*'. At this point in the agenda certain areas brought forward from the previous meeting will be dealt with. There may be matters to follow up from the previous meeting or supplementary reports to be given; these will be known in advance and accurate time planned for them. In addition there may be action points brought forward from the previous meeting. We will be looking at action points in more detail when we look at writing up the minutes, but essentially action points are those tasks which are given to particular team members to deal with and report back to at later meetings. Each of the people responsible will therefore present whatever results of their action they have and again this should be fairly easy to plan for.

There is a very important point in terms of effective planning here; suppose that a team member has been given the task of producing a particular report to put to the next meeting and arrives at that meeting not having done any of the work. Who is at fault here? The obvious answer would be the team member who has not completed the action given to them, but that is in fact only part of the story. Certainly that person is responsible for not having done the work, but there may be very good reasons why they have not. It is the meeting Secretary who is most at fault for not having found out beforehand that this action had not been dealt with. It may well be that this meeting has several people called to it who are no longer needed, because there is no report for them to follow up from and they could have been released for better planned time. Obviously, as a matter of courtesy, if team members know they have not completed their actions they can notify the Secretary, but responsibility must lie somewhere and unless otherwise stated it should be the Secretary's responsibility to contact the team members to ensure that all actions have been dealt with and that the planning of the subsequent agenda can be done effectively.

The next items to be listed on the agenda will be several *routine* items. Depending on the type of meeting you are holding, these may be 'reports of the treasurer', 'reports of the research sub-committee' etc. Presumably they arise at every meeting and they amount to updates of pure information flow. They can probably be dispensed with fairly quickly and should be timetabled to be dealt with as such, almost certainly needing little description as they will be well known to all members. However where there is any special amendment to any of these routine items of business this should be clearly spelt out so that all team members know that there is something else happening in this particular section.

As a general rule the next sections are the most important ones to get right in the agenda. These are the *non-routine items*. There is no point in putting a one-sentence heading on the agenda and expecting everybody to know what is expected of them. There is nothing wrong with putting one or more paragraphs under each of these headings to explain to all team members precisely what this heading is about, what is particularly expected of individuals or of the team generally and what the results of that section of the meeting are intended to be, i.e. whether there is to be a decision made, whether it is merely to be a review of position, whether a recommendation is required which can be put forward to others etc. The description should also clearly indicate what areas of subject matter are to be discussed and any ambiguity must be eliminated. More than in any other section of the agenda, the notes here amount to a briefing summary for the team members and if they are not clear then they are useless. One of the major faults of agendas is that they are usually all compressed on to one page and items usually only get one line at a time without any particular description. A great deal of corporate time is wasted when people come to meetings prepared to present what they believe is wanted, when in fact something quite different is expected of them.

The next heading on the agenda is '*Any other business*'. This is a subject of considerable debate; there is a school of thought that says that 'Any other business' should never appear on the agenda as this invariably means unplanned discussions, which are never as effective as planned discussions. On the other hand, we have seen all too many agendas which amount to nothing more than an introductory paragraph and then many hours of any other business. Neither position is to be recommended. Generally speaking, five or ten minutes can be allocated for any other business, and items which occur between the time of the agenda being distributed and the meeting itself can be brought up here. If they can be dealt with and polished off within the time then all well and good, you should allow this to avoid cluttering up future agendas. On the other hand, if they cannot be sorted out in that short period of time, then presumably they merit more discussion, and discussion is only effective if people have had time to plan for it. At this point, therefore, the item should be carried forward to a future agenda.

If the meeting is a regular meeting then the last item on the agenda should simply be a confirmation of the date, place and times (start and finish times) of the next meeting.

The minutes should be distributed shortly after the meeting and will give written forewarning of the next meeting. As the agenda may not be distributed for some time after that, given much of the criteria above, having the date, place and times of the meeting on the agenda also acts as a confirmation or a chance to notify members of any changes in the interim period. If there are changes to the date, place or times of the proposed meeting, it may well be advisable to highlight this fact on the agenda to ensure people change their diary notes.

All the above pre-planning of the meeting has two main effects and these cannot be overstated. First, people will feel good about meetings rather than regarding them as a drain on their time and being so energised will make proper use of meeting time rather than regarding them as a compulsory but unnecessary evil. Secondly, the net effect of all of the above proposals is that more people will have more time for other work. Some meetings will be replaced by other forms of communication, some people will not be called to meetings except for shorter periods, all meetings will run more expediently and in large organisations the work-hours saved in one year from even routine meetings can run into hundreds if not thousands. Valuable time. And time not to be wasted.

Check the validity of your meeting

The list of complaints about meetings ('I spend too long in meetings', 'I never get time to have a say', 'We have meetings when they are not necessary' and so on) are high among many people's complaints about company work. The checklist below is a valuable exercise in examining the validity of meetings you attend. It can be completed by any member of the team, but is most valuable if it is periodically completed by all members of the team (perhaps as an annual exercise). The possible results are discussed after the questions, but team leaders especially are advised to make summaries of all the team's responses and examine particularly the areas where there is some consensus as to particular success or difficulty. The corrective action which needs to be taken should then be clear, from the information in this chapter. Additionally, if one particular area (say, agendas) is highlighted as a problem, then the team leader might devise a small sub-questionnaire based on the information in this chapter to examine the problem in more detail. Alternatively, it might make an interesting subject for a brainstorm among members of the team.

The questions offer a range of compliance between one and six; with one as low (poor) compliance and six as high (effective, good) compliance. The higher the score, the more positive your feelings towards the subject of the question. Ring the number that most fits your belief about the question on that scale.

1. The team always knows the purpose of meetings and what is expected of it from the outset. 1 2 3 4 5 6

2. The team members are given the opportunity for effective preparation for meetings. 1 2 3 4 5 6

3. Agendas are always issued. 1 2 3 4 5 6

4. Agendas are clear and useful. 1 2 3 4 5 6

5. People turn up to meetings on time. 1 2 3 4 5 6

6. Meetings are well structured and well timed. 1 2 3 4 5 6

191

7. People at our meetings make valuable
   contributions.   1 2 3 4 5 6

8. I feel that I never spend time in meetings
   that is wasted or was not necessary.   1 2 3 4 5 6

9. The Chair actively asks for contributions
   and does not just accept only what is
   offered.   1 2 3 4 5 6

10. Discussion is well organised and
    controlled.   1 2 3 4 5 6

11. We reach effective decisions.   1 2 3 4 5 6

12. We rarely have to go back over old ground.   1 2 3 4 5 6

13. Our Chair distinguishes between what is
    urgent and what is important.   1 2 3 4 5 6

14. There is a great deal of enthusiasm for our
    meetings.   1 2 3 4 5 6

15. I feel able to contribute to discussions.   1 2 3 4 5 6

16. We do not hold meetings when other forms
    of communication (e.g. telephone, memos)
    would have been more appropriate.   1 2 3 4 5 6

17. Our meeting room/environment is con-
    ducive to good discussion and an open
    atmosphere.   1 2 3 4 5 6

18. Minutes of our meetings are distributed
    well in advance of next meetings.   1 2 3 4 5 6

19. Minutes are clear and accurate.   1 2 3 4 5 6

20. Action points are dealt with effectively and
    always followed up at meetings.   1 2 3 4 5 6

The minimum score possible on the checklist is 20 and the maximum is 120.

A score of 50 or below should give cause for concern as probably the whole culture of meetings is poorly thought out in your company.

Between 50 and 90 suggests that although meetings are running reasonably well, there are probably areas that could do with some fine-tuning; examine where the low results are coming from and address those areas as a priority.

A score of over 90 probably represents a very enlightened attitude to meetings; what is important is to see how that score moves up or down as you use the questionnaire on a series of occasions.

16. TEAMS: DEATH AND REBIRTH

'There is nothing permanent except change.'
Heraclitus

This chapter looks at how to end the team constructively when its useful life is over – many companies end up creating situations to service existing teams rather than simply removing the team.

Teams can end by:

- *reforming* into new teams for newly evolved goals, which have perhaps arisen from the successes of the team's previous efforts;
- *rejuvenating*, drawing in new blood and new resources in order that a 'worn out' team's efforts are not lost or wasted;
- *reincarnation*, where the team's purposes are fulfilled and the team is not needed, there must be use made of the experiences gained by the team members. Often they become valuable members of other teams, bringing in knowledge not just of their field of expertise, but also of team dynamics.

All teams are originally formed for a specific purpose and during the growth and development of the team – like a magnet drawing in iron filings – it will acquire new tasks and objectives; it may become a permanent part of the organisation. This need for self-perpetuation arises from the individual need for security.

If a team can sensibly demonstrate to the organisation that it has a clear role and is making an added value contribution to the business, it can continue to remain in place and justify its existence at all levels of the organisation.

However, some teams cannot demonstrate their continued usefulness and they then demand all the necessary support functions for the continuance of the team and fight for survival by removing all threats to its existence, often by acquiring the tasks that more properly should have gone to a new team.

How can the organisation correct such a situation? In some companies the new chief executive will simply, on arrival, disband the teams (often now called committees). This blunt removal is usually done without any in-depth planning and does not always analyse what these teams are doing, and subsequently can be disruptive to the organisation, as well as confusing the rest of the company. The further disadvantage of this 'machine-gun surgery' will usually mean that necessary tasks and projects will now have to be undertaken by individuals without the comfort and advice of their team members. This leads to an autocratic style of management in the short term. Without any structural change to back up the removal of teams they will – after licking their wounds – reform, informally or formally, into new teams and eventually the whole process will have to be gone through again.

What can managers do to circumnavigate this historical and continuing problem? One simple expedient is to install into the corporate culture the basic rule that teams do not have any divine right to remain in existence when their useful life is done. As Oliver Cromwell said to the Rump parliament in June 1654: 'It is not fit that you should sit here any longer! . . . You shall now give place to better men.'

It is our contention that it is the duty of the team leader and the individual team members to encourage themselves to get the job done and then voluntarily to wind themselves up. This, of course, has the added attraction of giving the team an awareness of their own destiny and further self-determination.

Another and obvious route is, at the outset of the team's formation, to decide a date (or at least aim at a date or set of criteria) when the team can feel that their job as a team has been accomplished. If necessary, publicise the fact that this team is only going to be in existence for a limited time. That way the organisation will instil in itself a sense of urgency to service the team with all the necessary resources, information etc. that it needs to achieve its objectives, one of which is now a deadline.

A more novel approach is to have a system of constantly expanding and contracting teams which – similar to musical chairs – swap about among themselves. In this instance individual team members may then realise that they have a great deal to contribute to the organisation through team work, and will welcome at every opportunity a challenge to work in new teams and on new projects through a process of self-rejuvenation.

Another similar version of this is not to allow contraction and expansion through an organic route, but have a retirement and removal system on a planned basis where, say, one-third to one-half of the team retire at a pre-determined date and then recruit new blood. Many teams, i.e. boards of directors, have some similar practices to this – often written into the company's fundamental 'rules', the articles and memorandum of association – but a change of 10 per cent or less annually is not a satisfactory approach to the problem. In fact, their reasons for doing this at all would only be for training or grooming a director for the future. Interestingly enough the removal or resignation is being sought of larger numbers of people from boards due to corporate mistakes and subsequent losses involved (e.g. Allied-Lyons).

We have in previous chapters discussed team roles, and we know that in any team an individual joining a team will choose a role to contribute to the whole. The problem can be that often the role is not that of first choice, but more of 'Last in, what's left for me?'. Every team player should have the opportunity at some stage in their development to demonstrate more than one role for the teams they are going to be working in. In many organisations human resources departments will identify and arrange such career moves for managers, but this process should be encouraged to go down the line into work groups to enable a wider range of experience by team forming and team stopping.

A more radical approach to the problem is for people in the organisation to refuse to delegate upwards any more tasks or objectives to the team. This 'sending-the-team-to-Coventry' method is very useful when dealing with teams comprised of senior managers of the organisation. Eventually, the members of the team will get the clear message that colleagues in the company do not see that they should remain in being, and unless they are very thick-skinned or extremely imaginative in thinking up things to do they will dissolve themselves.

We have, on many occasions, seen examples of this where the usefulness of very senior teams was not understood, or appreciated by middle management and, taking the bull by the horns, they slowly but surely stopped passing problems and decisions up the line and decided to solve the problems themselves. What in fact had happened here was that the team had been in existence for such a long time, and its decisions and the decision-making process was so visible, that they – by default – had actually trained middle management in their own image. In fairness to these teams, they saw what was happening, realised that this was positive and went along with it. In fact, the individual members of the team were so encouraged by what had happened that they started installing this process throughout the organisation and eventually it became a recognised part of the management structure.

How, then, can the manager recognise when a team has outlived its usefulness? This can often be done by a look into the minutes of the team meetings. For instance, take an example of a team that has been in existence for a long period of time. The obvious starting point is the first sets of minutes, to establish the following.

- Who was there; and how many?
- What departments did they represent?
- What was the purpose of the meeting?
- How many agenda items were dealt with?
- How long did the meeting last?
- How many actions were delegated to themselves?
- How many actions were referred to third parties?
- When did they agree to meet next?

Let's then move on to the current minutes and put down the same information, and record the changes. We can now see the current position.

- Who now attends the meeting and has the number of members increased or decreased?
- What departments have gone and what new ones have we gained?
- What is now the purpose of the meeting?
- How many agenda items are they now dealing with?
- How long is the meeting lasting now?
- How many actions are they now dealing with themselves?

197

- How many actions are they now delegating to third parties?
- When did they agree to meet next?

We can now award a points system to the information we have recorded.

- If the people who now attend the meeting have not substantially changed, but they have increased in numbers (co-opting to the team), award **no points**; if there have been substantial changes (i.e. new members and possibly a decrease in the numbers attending), award **one point**.
- If the departments represented have increased, award **no points**; if they have decreased, award **two points**.
- If the purpose of the meeting has not changed, award **no points**; if it has changed, award **one point**.
- If the number of constructive agenda items dealt with remained static or decreased, award **no points**; if the number has increased (by, say, 25 per cent), award **one point**.
- If the duration of the meeting remained constant or increased, award **no points**; if the length of the meeting has gone down (by, say, 25 per cent), award **two points**.
- If the number of actions delegated to themselves remained static or decreased, award **no points**; award **two points** if the number has increased by, say, 25 per cent.
- If the number of actions referred to third parties remained the same or increased, award **no points**; if the number has decreased, award **two points**.
- If they now meet at the same frequency or more often, award **no points**; if they meet less often, award **three points**.

The maximum points to be gained is therefore **fourteen**. If by this simple process the number of points gained is **seven** or less, you may wish to dissolve the team. If the number of points is **eight to fourteen**, then the team and the team members have grown organically into a different animal, and may well be fulfilling an important and added value contribution to the organisation.

Looking to the future

The farmer wisely does not leave seed corn to perish, he does not plough it over, and he does not consume or otherwise waste it.

The seed corn is there to be planted to grow the future crop. In teams there must be recognition that the team environment is the best place to develop good team members for other teams.

If reincarnation is one alternative end to the life of teams, as considered above, then there must be forward planning to facilitate this. Companies must not just wait for the right individuals to become available; they must be homegrown by planning the future needs of the business.

People are the seed corn of the organisation; demographic profiles and the awareness of skills shortages arising means that we must start again organically to grow our employees and our management. Too many of our organisations are graduate recruitment schools; we recruit, train and develop them, and eventually we hand over the running of our businesses to them. What, then, of the rest of our staff? We block certain promotable people at fixed levels in our organisations without any comprehension of the leadership and team contribution skills that may be lying fallow. What we are having to deal with here is the business feudal system. Most boards of directors are self-electing oligarchies who preach democracy, but practise participative autocracy through complicated chains of command, including matrix management. If, as we have mentioned before, people are our greatest asset, why do we not nurture these assets? Why – like the feudal system – are we only developing people of a certain class or background? If we want people to work in teams with all the advantages, why do we continue to reward the individual in secrecy behind closed doors? If we want to achieve teambuilding from our workforces, why do we prefer to acclaim and only recognise loners, who will often sacrifice team recognition in their preference for personal promotion? The examples of promoting teambuilding but dealing with and recognising individual effort are endless, and we do not need to trouble the reader with any more here.

We suspect that the root of the problem is in our schooling system. Most of our so-called 'good schools' still need to produce academic self-starters and achievers. Very little teambuilding is taught at our primary and secondary schools, apart from in sport, and where it is, it is usually badly done, causing parents to complain that their children are spending their time playing games and not concentrating on the three Rs. Group project work with eight or nine year olds is regarded as interesting but not pertinent in getting children into a 'decent school'. Business, commerce and our other institutions have to pick up what our schools give us, and business is always complaining at the result. But is not business also to blame; where is the input from business and commerce into our schooling systems, apart from the occasional gift of books or computers etc.?

Business must come clean on this; in order to survive against competition our organisations must create, build and nurture teams that know exactly what they are doing and why they are doing it. Teambuilding cannot be relegated only to the sports field, particularly in a society where loner sports, i.e. tennis, snooker, golf and darts yield the highest financial rewards.

What, as team leaders, managers and controllers, can we do? We have in previous chapters described teams, teambuilding and the reasons for team formation, but teambuilding is a philosophy, not a tool. We must as managers either accept that problems, opportunities and creative work are best dealt with by teams, with all the synergy and energy that teams can release, or we can continue with the Lone Ranger school of management. Teams, as we know, water down recognition for the individual, and possibly individual promotion prospects also. So why, then, are we surprised that under this system all that happens is that easy and high-profile decisions will be taken by individuals, and difficult ones and problematic and potentially awkward situations, will be delegated to a team so that blame can be apportioned when things go wrong?

Management must grow its people so that everyone has an equal chance of being developed to their full potential. This will mean putting a wider emphasis on training and less on the selection process. It will mean recognising that we are using only a small potential of the brain power of our employees, while pushing the select few, often beyond their intellectual capabilities. It also means that we must develop our employees so that they can achieve a better form of recognition from us than they are receiving at the present.

People like being in teams; it enables them to give air to their views, knowing that team members will filter out what is good for the team. Team work can be as rewarding as individual achievement and it is often more readily acceptable to other people in the organisation. There is a sense of achievement in doing things collectively; the loner will often appear more exciting as he or she seems to take the risk and the glory, but in business what risks do people really take, that at some point are not delegated to teams when trouble starts brewing?

Team players, including the team leader, leave something behind that is more permanent than just their reputations. They can take pride in the fact that they have now become surplus to the team, because they leave the team like a retiring teacher who has instilled into others the wherewithal to do the job or at the least the ability to ask the right questions and challenge the accepted positions so that the job can be furthered.

John Spencer and Adrian Pruss are principal trainers of APW Training.

APW Training can be contacted at:

The Leys
2c Leyton Road
Harpenden
Herts AL5 2TL

Telephone: (01582) 468592
Fax   : (01582) 461979

INDEX

Piatkus Business Books

Piatkus Business Books have been created for people like you, busy
executives and managers who need expert knowledge readily available in
a clear and easy-to-follow format. All the books are written by specialists
in their field. They will help you improve your skills quickly and
effortlessly in the workplace and on a personal level. Titles include:

General Management Skills

Be Your Own PR Expert Bill Penn
Brain Power: The 12-Week Mental Training Programme Marilyn vos Savant
  and Leonore Fleischer
The Complete Time Management System Christian H. Godefroy and
  John Clark
Confident Decision Making J. Edward Russo and Paul J. H. Schoemaker
Dealing with Difficult People Roberta Cava
The Energy Factor: How to Motivate Your Workforce Art McNeil
**Firing On All Cylinders: The Quality Management System for High-Powered
  Corporate Performance** Jim Clemmer with Barry Sheehy
How to Develop and Profit from Your Creative Powers Michael LeBoeuf
The Influential Manager: How to Use Company Politics Constructively
  Lee Bryce
Leadership Skills for Every Manager Jim Clemmer and Art McNeil
**Lure the Tiger Out of the Mountains – The 36 Stratagems of Ancient China:
  Timeless Tactics from the East for Today's Successful Manager** Gao Yuan
Managing Your Team John Spencer and Adrian Pruss
Memory Booster: Easy Techniques for Rapid Learning and a Better Memory
  Robert W. Finkel
Organise Yourself Ronni Eisenberg with Kate Kelly
**Play to Your Strengths: Focus on What You Do Well – and Success Will
  Follow** Donald O. Clifton and Paula Nelson
Problem Solving Techniques that Really Work Malcolm Bird
Quantum Learning: Unleasing the Genius Within You Bobbi DePorter
  and Mike Hernacki
The Successful Negotiator Christian H. Godefroy and Luis Robert

Sales and Customer Services

The Art of the Hard Sell Robert L. Shook
**Creating Customers: An Action Plan for Maximising Sales, Publicity and
  Promotion** David H. Bangs
How to Close Every Sale Joe Girard
How to Succeed in Network Marketing Leonard S. Hawkins
How to Win Customers and Keep Them for Life Michael LeBoeuf
Sales Power: The Silva Mind Method for Sales Professionals José Silva
  and Ed Bernd Jr
The Selling Edge: Tactics for Winning a Sale Every Time Patrick Forsyth
Telephone Selling Techniques that Really Work Bill Good

Presentation and Communication

Better Business Writing Maryann V. Piotrowski
The Complete Book of Business Etiquette Lynne Brennan and
  David Block

Confident Conversation: How to Talk in any Business or Social Situation
Dr Lillian Glass
He Says, She Says: Closing the Communication Gap Between the Sexes
Dr Lillian Glass
Personal Power: How to Achieve Influence and Success in Your Professional Life Philippa Davies
Powerspeak: The Complete Guide to Public Speaking and Communication
Dorothy Leeds
The Power Talk System: How to Communicate Effectively Christian H.
Godefroy and Stephanie Barrat
Say What You Mean and Get What You Want George R. Walther
Smart Questions for Successful Managers: A New Technique for Effective Communication Dorothy Leeds
Your Total Image: How to Communicate Success Philippa Davies

Careers

The Influential Woman: How to Achieve Success Without Losing Your Femininity Lee Bryce
Marketing Yourself: How to Sell Yourself and Get the Jobs You've Always Wanted Dorothy Leeds
Networking and Mentoring: A Woman's Guide Dr Lily Segerman-Peck
The Perfect CV Tom Jackson
Psychological Testing for Managers: A Complete Guide to Using and Surviving 19 Popular Recruitment and Career Development Tests Dr Stephanie Jones
10 Steps to the Top Marie Jennings
Which Way Now? How to Plan and Develop a Successful Career
Bridget Wright

Small Business

The Best Person for the Job Malcolm Bird
Creating Abundance: How to Bring Wealth and Fulfilment into Your Life
Andrew Ferguson
How to Collect the Money You Are Owed Malcolm Bird
Making Profits: A 6-Month Action Plan for the Small Business
Malcolm Bird
Perfectly Legal Tax Loopholes Stephen Courtney

For a free brochure with further information on our complete range of business titles, please write to:

Piatkus Books
Freepost 7 (WD 4505)
London W1E 4EZ

PIATKUS